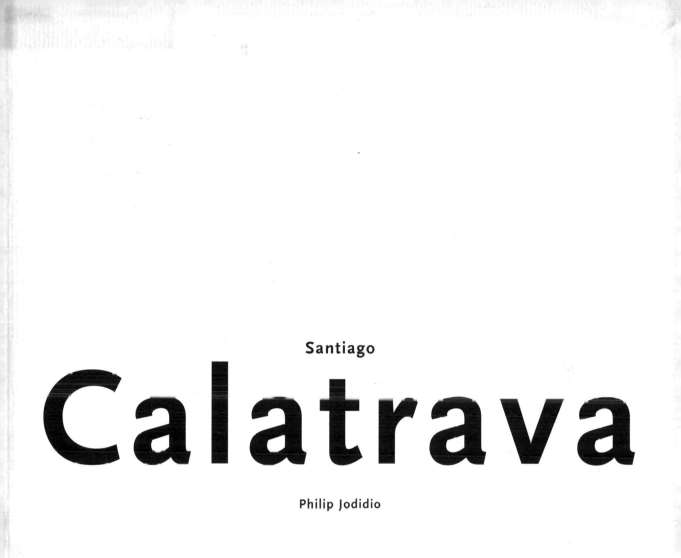

Santiago

Calatrava

Philip Jodidio

TASCHEN

KÖLN LONDON LOS ANGELES MADRID PARIS TOKYO

Acknowledgements > Remerciements > Danksagung

The publisher and author wish to thank Robertina
Calatrava as well as Kim Marangoni for their kind
assistance in the preparation of this book.

L'éditeur et l'auteur tiennent à remercier Robertina
Calatrava et Kim Marangoni pour leur soutien sur ce
projet de livre.

Der Verleger und der Autor danken Robertina Calatrava
ebenso wie Kim Marangoni für ihre freundliche
Unterstützung bei der Entstehung dieses Buches.

Front cover > Couverture > Umschlagvorderseite
Oriente Station, Lisbon, Portugal
© Photo: Christian Richters
Back cover > Dos de couverture > Umschlagrückseite
Lyon-Saint Exupéry Airport Railway Station, Lyon, France
© Santiago Calatrava
Page 1 > Seite 1
Portrait Santiago Calatrava, 1997
Photo: Luca Vignelli
Page 2 > Seite 2
Trinity Bridge, Salford, England (1993–1995)
Photo: John Edward Linden

© 2003 TASCHEN GmbH
Hohenzollernring 53, D–50672 Köln
www.taschen.com

Original edition: © 1998 Benedikt Taschen Verlag GmbH

Edited by Angela Pfotenhauer, Cologne
Design: Quim Nolla, [di'zain], Barcelona
German translation: Franca Fritz, Heinrich Koop, Straelen;
Annette Wiethüchter, Berlin
French translation: Jacques Bosser, Paris

Printed in Italy
ISBN 3–8228–2354–6

Contents > Sommaire > Inhalt

Santiago Calatrava is in many ways an unusual figure. Born in Spain in 1951, he studied art in Valencia before training there as an architect. More unexpected, he went on to study civil engineering at the Swiss Federal Institute of Technology (ETH) in Zurich. In 1981, he earned his doctorate there with a thesis concerning the "Foldability of Spaceframes". At a time when some well-known architects do not hesitate to proclaim that they are self-taught, Calatrava's background is, on the contrary, one of academic achievement. Speaking Spanish, English, French and German with almost equal fluency, crossing barriers between art, architecture and engineering as easily as he seems to change countries, Santiago Calatrava is clearly a figure to be reckoned with, a leading light of a generation that is now beginning to dominate world architecture.

The house near the shores of the Zurich-See that serves as both residence and office for Santiago Calatrava reveals a good deal about his character and working process. This solid stone dwelling can only be described as bourgeois from the outside, despite a number of Calatrava's sculptures that sit on the lawn. Within, the architect has rebuilt the structure, giving it a clean, modern aspect little disturbed by extraneous objects or clutter. An uninformed visitor might well conclude that this was the home and office not of an architect or engineer, but rather of a sculptor or painter. Few if any architectural drawings or even models are in evidence, whereas Calatrava's sculptures, drawings, furniture and lamps are omnipresent.

The relationship of Calatrava's works of art to his built designs is complex, even if some forms, such as the bird-like volume of his Lyon-Satolas TGV Station, are readily identifiable in his sculptures. "Sometimes, I create structural compositions, which you can call sculptures if you like," says Santiago Calatrava. "They are based on very personal ideas. Just as Fellini or Kurosawa made drawings before their movies, I make sculptures." Santiago Calatrava makes frequent references to art, and this is

A bien des égards, Santiago Calatrava est un personnage hors du commun. Né en Espagne en 1951, il fait des études artistiques puis d'architecture à Valence. De façon plus inattendue déjà, il part ensuite étudier l'ingénierie civil à l'Institut fédéral suisse de technologie (ETH) de Zurich. En 1981, il y passe son doctorat et soutient sa thèse sur le «Pliage des structures tridimensionnelles». À une époque où certains architectes célèbres n'hésitent pas à proclamer qu'ils sont autodidactes, la formation de Calatrava est on ne peut plus académique. Parlant avec presque la même aisance l'espagnol, l'anglais, le français et l'allemand, franchissant les frontières entre l'art, l'architecture et l'ingénierie aussi facilement qu'il change de pays, Santiago Calatrava est un personnage avec lequel il faut aujourd'hui compter, et l'un des chefs de file d'une génération qui commence à dominer l'architecture internationale.

La maison au bord du lac de Zurich qui lui sert à la fois de résidence et de bureau révèle en grande partie son caractère et sa méthode de travail. Cette construction en pierre massive pourrait être qualifiée de bourgeoise lorsqu'on la regarde de l'extérieur, malgré quelques sculptures de Calatrava disposées sur la pelouse. Mais l'architecte en a entièrement remodelé la structure intérieure, lui donnant un aspect net et moderne, à peine troublé par quelques objets étranges et un léger désordre. Un visiteur non informé pourrait penser qu'il s'agit plus de la maison et du lieu de travail d'un peintre ou d'un sculpteur que d'un architecte ou d'un ingénieur. On n'aperçoit guère de croquis ou de maquettes d'architecture, alors que ses sculptures, ses dessins, ses mobiliers et ses luminaires sont omniprésents.

La relation entre les œuvres artistiques de Calatrava et ses projets architecturaux est complexe, même si quelques formes, comme celle de sa gare de TGV de Lyon-Satolas qui rappelle un oiseau, pointent déjà dans ses sculptures. «Je crée parfois des compositions structurales que vous pouvez appeler sculptures si vous voulez,» précise-t-il. «Elles viennent d'idées qui me sont

The art of transgression   L'art de la tra

Santiago Calatrava ist in vielerlei Hinsicht eine ungewöhnliche Persönlichkeit der Architekturwelt. Er wurde 1951 in Spanien geboren und studierte in Valencia Kunst, bevor er in der gleichen Stadt sein Diplom als Architekt machte und sich im Anschluß daran seinem Bauingenieurstudium an der Eidgenössischen Technischen Hochschule (ETH) in Zürich widmete. 1981 promovierte Calatrava über das Thema: »Zur Faltbarkeit von Fachwerken«. In einer Zeit, in der einige berühmte Architekten stolz verkünden, daß sie Autodidakten seien, ist seine Laufbahn von akademischen Leistungen und Auszeichnungen geprägt. Calatrava, der Spanisch, Englisch, Französisch und Deutsch fast gleichermaßen fließend spricht und die Grenzen zwischen Kunst, Architektur und Ingenieurwesen mit ebensolcher Leichtigkeit überschreitet wie Ländergrenzen, gehört zu den bedeutendsten Persönlichkeiten unserer Zeit – und ist die Leitfigur einer Generation, die derzeit die Architekturwelt erobert.

Sein Wohnsitz in der Nähe des Zürich-Sees, der ihm als Wohn- und Bürogebäude dient, verrät einiges über Santiago Calatravas Charakter und seine Arbeitsmethoden. Das solide Steingebäude kann – trotz einiger Skulpturen Calatravas auf dem Rasen – von außen als konventionell bezeichnet werden. Im Inneren hat der Architekt die historische Villa jedoch völlig umgestaltet und ihr ein klares, modernes Erscheinungsbild gegeben, das kaum von persönlichem Kleinkram oder Unordnung gestört wird. Ein zufälliger Besucher könnte annehmen, daß dieses Anwesen eher einem angesehenen Maler oder Bildhauer gehören könnte als einem Architekten und Bauingenieur. Denn während sich im Inneren des Hauses nur wenige Bauzeichnungen oder architektonische Modelle finden, sind Calatravas Skulpturen, Zeichnungen, Möbel und Lampen allgegenwärtig.

Das Verhältnis zwischen Calatravas Kunstwerken und seinen gebauten Arbeiten ist recht komplex – auch wenn sich einige Formen, wie etwa der vogelähnliche Baukörper seines TGV-Bahnhofs Lyon-Satolas, in seinen Skulpturen leicht wiederfinden. »Manchmal schaffe ich strukturelle Kompositionen, die man, wenn man will, auch als Skulpturen bezeichnen kann«, erklärt Santiago Calatrava. »Sie beruhen auf sehr persönlichen Vorstellungen. So wie Fellini oder Kurosawa Zeichnungen anfertigten, bevor sie ihre Filme drehten, stelle ich Skulpturen her.« Calatravas häufige Bezüge zur Kunst sind sicherlich ein Schlüssel zu seinem Werk, was sich an seinem Haus in Zürich zeigt. »Eine Reihe von mir entworfener Brücken mit geneigtem Bogen könnte man vielleicht mit Cézannes Serie Les Baigneuses (Die Badenden) vergleichen«, erläutert er. »Die Kunst des 20. Jahrhunderts wurde stark beeinflußt von der marxistisch-leninistischen Auffassung von der Kunst für die Masse. Das ist jetzt vorbei. Wir finden allmählich wieder zurück zur Schaffensfreiheit, und das bedeutet neuen Raum für den Architekten als Künstler und für die Architektur als Kunst.«[1]

Santiago Calatrava scheint sich keine großen Gedanken über den jeweiligen Stellenwert der Architektur bzw. des Ingenieurwesens in der bebauten Umgebung oder auch in seinen eigenen

gression   Die Kunst der Transgression

undoubtedly one of the keys to his work, as is readily visible in the house in Zurich. "A series of bridges I designed with inclined arcs might be like Cézanne's series of 'Bathers'," he says. "The art of the twentieth century," he continues, "has been heavily influenced by the Marxist-Leninist concept of art for everyone. That is finished now. We are again finding the liberty to create, and this implies a new place for the architect as artist, and for architecture as art."[1]

Santiago Calatrava does not seem to be troubled greatly by the respective roles of architecture and engineering in the built environment, or indeed in his own work. As he says, "In principle, the architect is in charge, and the engineer works for him." And yet with his combined interests in art, engineering, and architecture, Calatrava is indeed close to the heart of one of the most intense debates in the recent history of construction and design. As Sigfried Giedion wrote in his seminal book *Space, Time and Architecture*, "The advent of the structural engineer with speedier, industrialized form-giving components broke up the artistic bombast and shattered the privileged position of the architect and provided the basis for present-day developments. The nineteenth-century engineer unconsciously assumed the role of guardian of the new elements he was continually delivering to the architects. He was developing forms that were both anonymous and universal." Giedion retraces the debate about the role of engineering by citing a number of essential dates and events. Amongst them, "1877: In this year the question entered the Académie, when a prize was offered for the best paper discussing 'the union or the separation of engineer and architect.' Davioud, one of the architects of the Trocadéro, won the prize with this answer: 'The accord will never become real, complete, and fruitful until the day that the engineer, the artist, and the scientist are fused together in the same person. We have for a long time lived under the foolish persuasion that art is a kind of activity distinct from all other forms of human intelligence, having its sole source

très personnelles. Comme Fellini ou Kurosawa faisaient des dessins avant leurs films, je réalise des sculptures.» Santiago Calatrava se réfère fréquemment à l'art, qui est certainement l'une des clés de son œuvre, comme on le constate dès sa maison zurichoise. «J'ai conçu une série de ponts à arches inclinées qui pourrait être comparée à celle des Baigneuse de Cézanne,» fait-il remarquer. «L'art du XXe siècle a été lourdement influencé par le concept marxiste-léniniste de l'art pour tous. Tout ceci est fini aujourd'hui. Nous retrouvons enfin la liberté de créer, ce qui implique une nouvelle place pour l'architecte en tant qu'artiste, et pour l'architecture en tant qu'art.»[1]

Il ne semble pas réellement préoccupé par les rôles respectifs de l'architecte et de l'ingénieur dans le processus de construction, pas plus que dans sa propre recherche. «En principe, l'architecte est responsable, et l'ingénieur travaille pour lui.» dit-il. Néanmoins, à travers l'intérêt qu'il manifeste à la fois pour l'art, l'ingénierie et l'architecture, Calatrava se retrouve concrètement au cœur de l'un des débats les plus animés de l'histoire récente de la construction et de la conception. Comme l'écrit Sigfried Giedion dans son livre majeur, *Espace, temps et architecture*: «L'arrivée de l'ingénieur spécialisé dans le champ de la structure, armé de techniques industrialisées et plus rapides de recherches formelles, a fait éclater la boursouflure artistique, mis en pièce la position privilégiée de l'architecte, et donné une base nouvelle aux développements actuels. L'ingénieur du XIXe siècle remplissait inconsciemment le rôle de garant des éléments de nouveauté qu'il apportait aux architectes. Il mettait au point des formes à la fois anonymes et universelles.» Giedion retrace le débat sur le rôle de l'ingénierie en citant quelques dates essentielles. Parmi elles : «1877 : cette année là, la question fit son entrée à l'Académie lorsqu'un prix fut proposé pour la meilleure communication sur le thème de l'union ou de la séparation de l'ingénieur et de l'architecte. Davioud, l'un des architectes du Trocadéro, remporta la distinction avec cette

Arbeiten zu machen. »Im Prinzip«, so erläutert er, »trägt der Architekt die Verantwortung, und der Bauingenieur arbeitet für ihn.« Dennoch bewegt er sich – mit seinem gleichermaßen ausgeprägten Interesse an Kunst, Ingenieurbau und Architektur – im Zentrum einer der heftigsten Debatten in der jüngsten Geschichte des Bauwesens und Designs sehr nahe. Sigfried Giedion schrieb dazu 1941 in seinem zukunftsweisenden Buch *Raum, Zeit und Architektur: Die Entstehung einer neuen Tradition*: »Das Aufkommen des Statikers und der schnelleren, industrialisierten, formbestimmenden Bauelemente bereitete dem künstlerischen Überschwang ein Ende, zerstörte die privilegierte Position des Architekten und bildete die Basis für die heutigen Entwicklungen. Der Bauingenieur des 19. Jahrhunderts übernahm unbewußt die Rolle eines Wächters über diese neuen Elemente, die er den Architekten fortlaufend an die Hand lieferte. Er entwickelte Formen, die zugleich anonym und universell waren.« Giedion rekonstruiert die Debatte über die Rolle des Ingenieurwesens, indem er eine Reihe wichtiger Daten und Ereignisse aufführt: »1877: Die Akademie stellt eine Preisfrage über *L'union ou la separation des ingénieurs et des architectes* (*Die Einheit oder Trennung von Ingenieur und Architekt*). Davioud, der Architekt des Trocadéro, erhält den Preis mit der Beantwortung ›Die Vereinigung zwischen Architekt und Ingenieur muß untrennbar sein. Die Lösung wird erst dann wirklich, vollständig und fruchtbar sein, wenn Architekt und Ingenieur, Künstler und Wissenschaftler, in einer Person vereinigt sind ... Wir leben seit langem in der einfältigen Überzeugung, daß die Kunst eine Wesenheit sei, die sich von allen anderen Formen der menschlichen Intelligenz unterscheide, durchaus unabhängig habe sie ihre Quellen und ihre einzige Geburtsstätte in der kapriziösen Phantasie der Künstlerpersönlichkeit.‹«[2] Obwohl weder Giedions Beharren auf der »Anonymität« der Arbeit des Ingenieurs noch Daviouds Verweis auf die »launenhaften Einfälle« des Künstlers zu Santiago Calatravas kraftvollem, originellen und schöpferischen Charakter passen wollen, scheint er der Forderung des Franzosen nach einer Einigung von Ingenieurbau und Architektur gerecht zu werden.

DIE TRADITION DER INGENIEURE UND KÜNSTLER

Der Katalog zu Calatravas Ausstellung im Museum of Modern Art in New York (1993) hebt die enge Verbindung seiner Werke zu den Arbeiten anderer wegweisender Ingenieure hervor: »Calatrava steht in der Tradition des Ingenieurbaus im 20. Jahrhundert. Wie die Vertreter der vorhergehenden Generation – Robert Maillart, Pier Luigi Nervi, Eduardo Torroja und Félix Candela – geht Calatrava weit über ein Konzept hinaus, das sich lediglich mit der Lösung technischer Probleme beschäftigt. Für diese Ingenieure stellt ein Baukörper ein Gleichgewicht zwischen dem wissenschaftlichen Kriterium der Effizienz und der Schaffung neuer Formen dar. Calatrava betrachtet den Ingenieurbau als ›Kunst des Möglichen‹ und strebt nach einer neuen Formensprache, die auf technischem Know-how basiert und dennoch kein Loblied auf die Technologie darstellt.«[3] Der erste der erwähnten

< Campo Volantin Footbridge, Bilbao, Spain
> Bach de Roda–Felipe II, Barcelona, Spain

and origin in the personality of the artist himself and in his capricious fancy.'"[2] Though neither Giedion's insistence on the "anonymity" of the work of the engineer nor Davioud's reference to the "capricious fancy" of the artist seem to fit well with Calatrava's powerful originality, he does appear to meet the Frenchman's requirements for an accord between engineering and architecture.

THE HERITAGE OF ENGINEERS AND ARTISTS

The catalogue of Calatrava's 1993 exhibition at the Museum of Modern Art in New York underlines the close relationship of his work to that of other ground-breaking engineers: "Calatrava is part of the distinguished heritage of twentieth century engineering. Like those of the preceding generations – Robert Maillart, Pier Luigi Nervi, Eduardo Torroja, and Félix Candela – Calatrava goes beyond an approach that merely solves technical problems. Structure, for these engineers, is a balance between the scientific criterion of efficiency and the innovation of new forms. Calatrava considers engineering 'the art of the possible,' and seeks a new vocabulary of form that is based on technical know-how, yet is not an anthem to techniques."[3] The first figure cited, Robert Maillart (1872–1940), graduated from the ETH in Zurich in 1894 and went on to create some of the most spectacular modern bridges, and to make innovative use of concrete. His Giesshübel Warehouse in Zurich (1910) employed a concrete slab "mushroom ceiling" for the first time, permitting Maillart to do away with the use of beams. As Matilda McQuaid writes: "Maillart was one of the first engineers of this century to break completely from masonry construction and apply a technically appropriate and elegant solution to reinforced concrete construction. Although the technical idea in Calatrava's work is neither the primary motivation, as with Maillart, nor understated, it informs the overall expression of the structure. His work becomes an 'intertwinement of plastic expression and structural revelation,

réponse : 'L'accord ne sera jamais réel, complet et fructueux tant que l'ingénieur, l'artiste et le savant n'auront pas fusionné dans la même personne. Pendant une longue période, nous avons vécu sous la conviction absurde que l'art était un type d'activité distincte de toutes les autres formes de l'intelligence humaine, trouvant ses seules sources et origines dans la personnalité de l'artiste lui–même et les caprices de son imagination.»[2] Bien que ni l'instance de Giedion sur «l'anonymat» de l'œuvre de l'ingénieur, ni la référence de Davioud aux «caprices de l'imagination» de l'artiste ne semblent réellement convenir à la puissante originalité de Calatrava, celui-ci pourrait bien matérialiser aujourd'hui la prédiction de l'architecte français sur l'accord entre l'ingénierie et l'architecture.

L'HÉRITAGE DES INGÉNIEURS ET DES ARTISTES

Le catalogue de l'exposition de Calatrava au Museum of Modern Art de New York (1993) souligne l'étroite relation entre son œuvre et celle d'autres grands ingénieurs précurseurs : «Calatrava appartient au patrimoine le plus remarquable de l'ingénierie du XXe siècle. Comme les grands maîtres des générations précédentes – Robert Maillart, Pier Luigi Nervi, Eduardo Torroja et Félix Candela – il va au-delà d'une approche qui se contenterait de résoudre des problèmes techniques. Pour ces ingénieurs, la structure résulte d'un équilibre entre le critère scientifique d'efficacité et l'innovation dans la recherche formelle. Calatrava considère l'ingénierie comme 'l'art du possible', et recherche un vocabulaire formel nouveau reposant sur un savoir-faire technologique, qui n'est pas pour autant un hymne à la technique.»[3] Le premier cité, Robert Maillart (1872–1940), diplômé de l'ETH de Zurich en 1894, a créé quelques uns des ponts les plus spectaculaires de l'époque moderne, et utilisé le béton de manière innovatrice. Son entrepôt de Giesshübel (Zurich, 1910) utilise pour la première fois un plafond en dalle champignon de béton, qui lui permet de se passer d'une poutraison. Comme

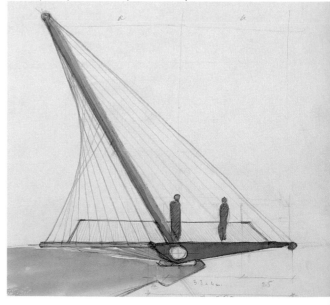

Bauingenieure, Robert Maillart (1872–1940), beendete 1894 sein Studium an der ETH in Zürich und schuf später einige der richtungsweisenden Brücken des zwanzigsten Jahrhunderts, bei denen er Beton auf innovative Weise einsetzte. Bei seinem Lagerhaus für die Zürcher Gesellschaft in Zürich-Giesshübel (1910) wandte er erstmals die von ihm entwickelte Pilzdecken-Konstruktion an, die es ihm ermöglichte, auf die Verwendung von Stützen und Balken zu verzichten. Matilda McQuaid schrieb dazu: »Maillart war einer der ersten Ingenieure dieses Jahrhunderts, der konsequent mit dem Mauerwerkbau brach und eine technisch angemessene und elegante Lösung zur Verstärkung von Betonkonstruktionen zum Einsatz brachte. Obwohl der technische Aspekt in Calatravas Werk weder vorrangiges Ziel – wie bei Maillart – noch völlig untergeordnet ist, prägt er den Gesamteindruck der Konstruktion. Seine Arbeiten werden zu einer ›Verflechtung von anschaulicher Ausdrucksform und struktureller Offenbarung, wobei Ergebnisse entstehen, die man wahrscheinlich am besten als Synthese von Ästhetik und Bauphysik beschreiben kann.‹«[4]

Obwohl er Maillarts Werke bewundert, legt Santiago Calatrava Wert darauf, daß sich seine Brücken deutlich von denen seines Vorbilds unterscheiden – und sei es nur durch ihre Lage. »Maillarts Brücken«, erklärt er, »sind häufig umgeben von einer wunderschönen Berglandschaft. Sein Verdienst bestand darin, ein künstliches Element auf gelungene Weise in eine so großartige Umgebung zu integrieren. Heute dagegen zählt meines Erachtens die Beschäftigung mit den Randgebieten der großen Städte zu den wichtigsten Aufgaben. Sehr häufig sind die staatlich geförderten Bauten in diesen Gebieten rein funktional; und doch können Brücken sogar in der Nähe von Bahngleisen oder bei der Überbrückung von verschmutzten Flüssen eine erstaunlich positive Wirkung erzielen. Indem sie eine ansprechende Umgebung schaffen, üben sie einen symbolischen Einfluß aus, dessen Auswirkungen weit über den unmittelbaren Standort hinausgehen.«[5]

Calatravas Werke sind zweifellos von den Arbeiten Felix Candelas beeinflußt, der 1910 in Madrid geboren wurde und 1939 nach Mexiko auswanderte, wo er eine Reihe bemerkenswerter Schalenbaukonstruktionen errichtete, darunter auch die Iglesia de la Virgen Milagrosa (Navarte, Mexiko, 1955) – ein Entwurf, der vollständig auf hyperbolischen Paraboloiden basiert. Ein anderer Spanier, der in Madrid geborene Bauingenieur Eduardo Torroja (1899–1961), war fasziniert von der Verwendung organischer oder vegetativer Formen, deren skulpturales Erscheinungsbild möglicherweise auf den Einfluß Gaudís zurückgeht. Matilda McQuaid erklärt hierzu, daß sich Calatrava in seinen Werken oft auf spanische – und insbesondere auf katalonische – Architekten und Künstler bezieht. Nicht zufällig gilt Malern und Bildhauern seine größte Bewunderung. »Was mich beispielsweise an Goya fasziniert«, sagt Calatrava, »ist die Tatsache, daß er zu den ersten Künstlern zählte, die sich – wie schon Rembrandt – von der Vorstellung lösten, allen Herren dienen zu müssen. Und was ich an Mirós Werken besonders bewundere, ist ihre bemerkenswerte Stille und die rigorose

< Campo Volantin Footbridge, Bilbao, Spain
> Trinity Bridge, Salford, England

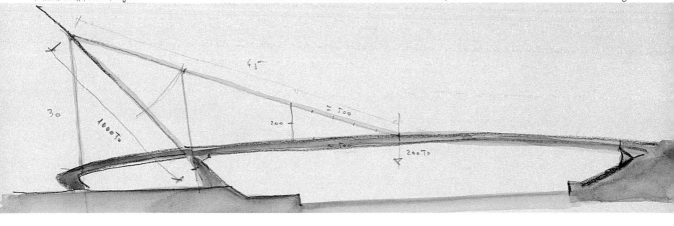

producing results that possibly can be best described as a synthesis of aesthetics and structural physics.'"[4]

Although he naturally admires the work of Maillart, Santiago Calatrava is quick to point out that his bridges are very different from those of his predecessor, if only because of their sites. "Maillart's bridges," says Calatrava, "are often set in beautiful mountain scenery. His achievement was to successfully introduce an artificial element into such magnificent locations. Today," he continues, "I believe that one of the most important tasks is to reconsider the periphery of cities. Most often public works in such areas are purely functional, and yet even near railroad tracks, or spanning polluted rivers, bridges can have a remarkably positive effect. By creating an appropriate environment they can have a symbolic impact whose ramifications go far beyond their immediate location."[5]

Calatrava's work has undoubtedly been influenced by that of Félix Candela, who was born in Madrid in 1910, and emigrated to Mexico in 1939, where he created a number of remarkable thin-shelled concrete structures such as the Iglesia de la Virgen Milagrosa (Navarte, Mexico, 1955), a design based entirely on hyperbolic paraboloids. Another Spaniard, the Madrid engineer Eduardo Torroja (1900–1961) was fascinated by the use of organic or vegetal forms whose undeniable sculptural presence may well spring from the influence of Gaudí. As Matilda McQuaid points out, despite Calatrava's being based in Zurich, many of his references are to Spanish, and more specifically to Catalan, architects or artists. Indeed, it seems to be no accident that he most admires painters and sculptors. "What fascinates me in the personality of Goya, for example," says Calatrava, "is that he is one of the first artists to renounce the idea, as Rembrandt had before him, of serving any one master. What I admire in Miro's work," he continues, "is its remarkable silence, as well as his radical rejection of everything conventional." Although Gaudí provides him with an example, as does Maillart,

l'écrit Matilda McQuaid : «Maillart a été l'un des premiers ingénieurs de ce siècle à rompre complètement avec la maçonnerie, et à appliquer une technique appropriée et des solutions élégantes à la construction en béton armé.»[4]

Si la recherche conceptuelle technique n'est pas la première motivation de Calatrava, mais ne doit pas être minorée pour autant, elle nourrit l'expression globale de ses structures. Son œuvre devient ainsi un «entrelacement d'expression plastique et de mise en valeur structurelle, produisant des résultats que l'on peut à juste titre décrire comme une synthèse d'esthétique et physique structurelle.»

Bien qu'il admire tout naturellement l'œuvre de Maillart, Santiago Calatrava s'empresse de faire remarquer que ses ponts sont très différents de ceux de son prédécesseur, ne serait-ce que par leur site. «Les ponts de Maillart,» dit-il, «sont souvent situés dans un magnifique paysage montagneux. Sa gloire a été de réussir à introduire des éléments artificiels dans des lieux splendides. Aujourd'hui, je pense que l'une des tâches les plus importantes est de reprendre en main la périphérie des villes. La plupart du temps, les travaux réalisés par les collectivités dans ces zones sont d'ordre purement fonctionnel, alors que même situés près de voies de chemin de fer ou franchissant des voies d'eau polluées, les ponts peuvent exercer un effet remarquablement positif. En créant un environnement approprié, ils sont en mesure d'offrir un impact symbolique dont les ramifications vont bien au-delà de leur site immédiat.»[5]

L'œuvre de Calatrava est sans aucun doute marquée par celle de Félix Candela, qui, né à Madrid en 1910, émigre au Mexique en 1939, où il construit un certain nombre de remarquables structures à voile mince en béton, telles l'église de la Virgen Milagrosa (Navarte, Mexique, 1955), entièrement à base de paraboloïdes hyperboliques. Durant la même période, un autre Espagnol, l'ingénieur madrilène Eduardo Torroja (1900–1961), est fasciné par les formes organiques ou végétales, dont la présence

Maquete nº ① pavillon flotante sobre el lago
Lucerna

Calatrava seems to be more at ease speaking about an artist such as the sculptor Julio Gonzalez.

"The father and grandfather of Gonzalez were metalworkers for Gaudí on projects like the Parque Guell. Then they went to Paris, and that is where the work of Julio Gonzalez with metal comes from. With all due modesty," concludes Calatrava, "one might say that what we do is a natural continuation of the work of Gaudí and of Gonzalez, a work of artisans moving toward abstract art."[6]

The kind of art that Santiago Calatrava is referring to is apparent in his most successful bridges and buildings, and yet it remains difficult to describe in words. Another of the essential figures of twentieth century engineering, the Italian Pier Luigi Nervi attempted such a definition in a series of lectures he delivered at Harvard in 1961: "It is very difficult to explain the reason for our immediate approval of forms which come to us from a physical world with which we, seemingly, have no direct tie whatsoever. Why do these forms satisfy and move us in the same manner as natural things such as flowers, plants, and landscapes to which we have become accustomed through numberless generations? It can also be noted that these achievements have in common a structural essence, a necessary absence of all decoration, a purity of line and shape more than sufficient to define an authentic style, a style I have termed the truthful style. I realize how difficult it is to find the right words to express this concept."

Calatrava: "When I make these remarks to friends, I am often told that this view of the near future is terribly sad, that perhaps it would be better to renounce voluntarily the further tightening of the bonds between our creations and the physical laws, if indeed these ties must lead us to a fatal monotony. I do not find this pessimism justified. Binding as technical demands may be there always remains a margin of freedom sufficient to show the personality of the creator of a work and, if he be an artist, to allow that his creation, even in its strict technical obedience, become a real and true work of art."[7]

sculpturale indéniable vient peut–être de l'influence de Gaudí. Comme le fait remarquer Matilda McQuaid, si Calatrava travaille à Zurich, beaucoup de ses références sont espagnoles ou plus spécifiquement liées à des architectes et artistes catalans. Ce n'est pas un hasard s'il admire particulièrement les peintres et les sculpteurs. «Ce qui me fascine dans la personnalité de Goya, par exemple,» dit-il, «c´est qu'il soit l'un des rares artistes à renoncer – comme Rembrandt avant lui – à l'idée de servir un quelconque maître. J'admire chez Miró son remarquable silence, et son rejet radical de toute convention.» Bien que Gaudí lui fournisse – ainsi que Maillart – un exemple, il semble être plus à l'aise pour parler d'un artiste comme le sculpteur Julio Gonzalez. «Le père et le grand-père de Gonzalez étaient des métalliers qui travaillaient pour Gaudí et intervinrent sur des projets comme le Parc Güell. Puis, ils s'installèrent à Paris, et c'est là l'origine des recherches de Julio Gonzalez sur le métal. En toute modestie,» conclut l'architecte, «on pourrait dire que ce que nous faisons est la continuation naturelle de l'œuvre de Gaudí et de Gonzalez, un travail d'artisans évoluant vers l'art abstrait.»[6]

La forme de création artistique à laquelle se réfère l'architecte est particulièrement évidente dans ses ponts les plus réussis, mais n'en reste pas moins difficile à décrire par les mots. Une autres des grandes figures fondamentales de l'ingénierie du XXᵉ siècle, l'Italien Pier Luigi Nervi, tenta de la définir lors d'une série de conférences donnée à Harvard en 1961 : «Il est difficile d'expliquer la raison pour laquelle nous approuvons instantanément des formes qui nous viennent d'un monde physique avec lequel nous n'avons apparemment aucune sorte de lien direct. Pourquoi ces formes nous satisfont-elles et nous émeuvent-elles de la même manière que les objets de la nature, tels les paysages, les plantes et les fleurs auxquels nous sommes habitués depuis des générations ? On doit aussi noter que ces accomplissements possèdent en commun une essence structurelle, une absence nécessaire de tout ornement, une

Ablehnung alles Konventionellen.« Obwohl ihm Gaudí und Maillart Vorbilder und Anregungen lieferten, spricht Calatrava lieber über Künstler wie den Bildhauer Julio Gonzalez. »Gonzalez' Vater und Großvater waren als Metallverarbeiter für Gaudí an Projekten wie dem Parco Güell tätig. Anschließend gingen sie nach Paris. Vor diesem Hintergrund entstanden Julio Gonzalez' Werke in Metall. Bei aller Bescheidenheit«, resümiert Calatrava, »könnte man sagen, daß es sich bei dem, was wir machen, um eine natürliche Fortsetzung der Arbeit von Gaudí und Gonzalez handelt, der Arbeit von Kunsthandwerkern, die sich der abstrakten Kunst annähert.«[6]

Die Kunstform, auf die Santiago Calatrava anspielt, kommt in seinen gelungensten Brücken und Bauwerken zum Ausdruck, und dennoch fällt es schwer, sie in Worte zu fassen. Eine andere bedeutende Persönlichkeit des Ingenieurbaus im 20. Jahrhundert, der Italiener Pier Luigi Nervi, bemühte sich 1961 in seiner Vorlesungsreihe an der Harvard University um eine solche Definition: »Der Grund für unsere unmittelbare Bewunderung für bestimmte Formen, die aus der physikalischen Welt stammen, zu der wir scheinbar keine direkte Verbindung haben, läßt sich nur schwer erklären. Warum befriedigen und bewegen uns diese Formen auf ähnliche Weise wie natürliche Dinge – Blumen, Pflanzen und Landschaften, an die wir uns bereits vor zahllosen Generationen gewöhnt haben? Es sollte auch darauf hingewiesen werden, daß diese Errungenschaften eine strukturelle Wesensart gemein haben, nämlich das notwendige Fehlen aller Verzierungen, eine Klarheit der Linien und Formen, die zur Definition eines unverfälschten Stils mehr als genügt – eines Stils, den ich als wahrhaften Stil bezeichne. Dabei ist mir durchaus bewußt, wie schwer es fällt, die richtigen Worte zur Erläuterung dieses Konzepts zu finden.«

Dazu Calatrava: »Wenn ich mit Freunden über dieses Konzept spreche, wird mir oft gesagt, daß diese Sicht der nahen Zukunft furchtbar trist sei und daß es vielleicht besser wäre, freiwillig auf eine Annäherung unserer Werke an die Naturgesetze zu verzichten, wenn diese Beziehungen tatsächlich zu einer tödlichen Monotonie führen. Ich halte diesen Pessimismus nicht für gerechtfertigt. So sehr die technischen Anforderungen uns auch binden, es bleibt doch immer noch ein Rest Freiheit übrig, der ausreicht, die Persönlichkeit des Urhebers einer Arbeit sichtbar zu machen, und der es möglich macht, daß das Werk eines Künstlers – selbst unter strikter Beachtung technischer Anforderungen – zu einem wahren Kunstwerk wird.«[7]

DIE DIALEKTIK DER TRANSGRESSION

Der Grund dafür, daß Calatrava seit zwanzig Jahren in Zürich lebt, liegt in den damaligen Umständen: Nach Beendigung seines Studiums blieb er in der Stadt, weil seine aus Schweden stammende Frau Robertina ihr Studium noch nicht beendet hatte. Wie es der Zufall wollte, gewann er 1982 die offene Ausschreibung für den neuen Bahnhof Stadelhofen (1982–90). Zu sagen, daß sich dieses ungewöhnliche Bauwerk in zentraler Lage befindet, wäre fast eine Untertreibung. Der Bahnhof grenzt

< Stadelhofen Railway Station, Zurich, Switzerland
> Stadelhofen Railway Station, Zurich, Switzerland

A DIALECTIC OF TRANSGRESSION

The reason for Calatrava's continued presence in Zurich is one of circumstances. Having completed his own studies, he stayed on there because his wife, Robertina, who is of Swedish origin, had not yet completed hers. Then, as luck would have it, he won a 1982 open competition to design the new Stadelhofen Railway Station (1982–90). To say that this unusual building is centrally located would almost be an understatement. Set into a green hill near Bellevue-Platz and off Theater-Strasse close to the lake, it is tightly integrated into a largely traditional urban environment. "In order to understand the Stadelhofen Railway Station," says Santiago Calatrava, "you have to view it as an extremely urban project, one that entailed the repair of the urban fabric. There is a clear contrast between the radical nature of the technical and architectural solutions chosen, and the attitude toward the city, which is extremely gentle. Any number of links have been created – not only bridges and access points, but connections with the streets that didn't exist before. Small park areas such as the veil of greenery hanging over the upper level were created." Indeed, when approaching the station from the city, the visitor first encounters a very traditional pavilion, which originally housed the station, before entering or descending into the areas designed specifically by Calatrava. "It was obvious from the outset," continues the architect, "that the respect given to buildings over a hundred years old in Switzerland precluded any attempt to demolish or substantially modify the old station house. I did not find that aspect illogical, however, because it fits into a reading of the city that remains intact."[8] Once the traveler has gone past the old pavilion, however, he enters a very different world, which seems closer to the imagination of Gaudí than to that of the stolid burghers of Zurich. Although Calatrava points out that Zurich does have something of a tradition of radical architecture with houses by figures such as Marcel Breuer, it is clear that with the Stadelhofen Station he indulged for the first time in his career

pureté de ligne et de forme plus que suffisantes pour définir un style authentique, que j'ai appelé le style véridique. Je réalise à quel point il est difficile de trouver les mots exacts pour exprimer ce concept.» «Lorsque je fais ces remarques à des amis, ils me répondent souvent que cette vision du proche futur est terriblement attristante, et qu'il serait peut-être mieux de renoncer volontairement à un nouveau resserrement de ces liens entre nos créations et les lois physiques, s'il apparaît qu'ils devaient nous conduire à une monotonie fatale. Je ne pense pas que ce pessimisme soit justifié. Aussi contraignantes que puissent être les exigences techniques, il reste toujours une marge de liberté suffisante pour permettre à la personnalité du créateur d'une œuvre de s'affirmer, et, s'il est un artiste, de permettre à cette création, même dans son strict respect de la technique, de devenir une œuvre d'art réelle et véridique.»[7]

UNE DIALECTIQUE DE TRANSGRESSION

La raison de la présence de Calatrava à Zurich relève des circonstances. Après avoir achevé ses études, il choisit d'y demeurer pour sa femme d'origine suédoise, Robertina, qui n'y avait pas encore achevé les siennes. Puis, signe du destin, il remporte en 1982 un concours pour la nouvelle gare de chemin de fer de Stadelhofen (1982–90). Ce curieux bâtiment ne pourrait être plus central. Implanté au flanc d'une colline de verdure près de Bellevue-Platz et non loin de la Theater-Strasse et du lac, il est étroitement intégré à un environnement urbain essentiellement traditionnel. «Pour comprendre cette gare,» explique Calatrava, «vous devez la voir comme un projet extrêmement urbain, l'une de ces interventions qui contribuent à la remise en état du tissu urbain. Elle présente un contraste très marqué entre le radicalisme de la solution technique et architecturale retenue et l'attitude envers la ville qui est toute d'attention. De multiples liens ont été créés – non seulement des ponts et des points d'accès, mais même des connexions avec des rues, qui n'existaient pas

an eine geschwungene, abschüssige Grünfläche in der Nähe des Bellevue–Platzes und der Theaterstraße. Er ist fest in eine größtenteils traditionelle städtische Umgebung integriert. »Um den Bahnhof Stadelhofen zu verstehen«, erklärt Santiago Calatrava, »muß man ihn als ein urbanes Projekt betrachten, das eine Reparatur der städtischen Struktur nach sich zieht. Der Bau markiert einen deutlichen Kontrast zwischen der radikalen technischen und architektonischen Lösung und der ausgesprochen versöhnlichen Haltung zu seiner städtischen Umgebung. Es wurden zahlreiche Verbindungen geschaffen – nicht nur Brücken und Anschlußbauwerke, sondern auch neue Verbindungen zu den umliegenden Straßen sowie kleine Parkflächen wie etwa die Grünanlage, die sich über die obere Ebene erstreckt.« Nähert man sich Calatravas Bau von der Stadt aus, so trifft man zunächst auf das alte Bahnhofsgebäude, bevor man die von Calatrava entworfenen Bereiche betritt. »Es war ganz offensichtlich«, fährt der Architekt fort, »daß jeder Versuch, das alte Bahnhofsgebäude abzureißen oder grundlegend zu verändern, von vornherein zum Scheitern verurteilt sein würde, da man hier in der Schweiz über einhundert Jahre alten Bauwerken großen Respekt zollt. Diese Haltung finde ich sehr nachvollziehbar, denn sie paßt zur Auffassung von der Stadt als intakter Einheit.«[8] Sobald der Besucher jedoch das alte Gebäude hinter sich läßt, betritt er eine völlig andere Welt, die den Phantasieschöpfungen Gaudís bedeutend näher kommt als der ruhigen Gleichmut der angestammten Zürcher Architektur. Obwohl Calatrava darauf hinweist, daß Zürich auf eine gewisse Tradition moderner Architektur zurückblicken kann (mit Häusern von Architekten wie Marcel Breuer), ist es offensichtlich, daß er mit dem Bahnhof Stadelhofen zum ersten Mal in seiner Laufbahn die für ihn charakteristische innovative Gestaltung auch in großem Maßstab ausführte.

Der neue Bahnhof – einschließlich eines großen Einkaufszentrums im Untergeschoß – entstand auf einem geschwungenen, 40 x 240 Meter großen Gelände, während der Betrieb der Pendlerzüge aufrechterhalten werden mußte. Der Entwurf zeichnet sich durch eine organische Einheit aus, die angesichts der Umstände nicht schlichter hätte ausfallen können. Calatravas Konstruktion läßt an einen Flugsaurier denken, der sich auf diesem Hügel niedergelassen hat, und sie ist durch ein Muster sich wiederholender Elemente gegliedert: Riesige anthropomorphe Eingangstore führen zum unterirdischen Einkaufszentrum, in dem der Besucher den Eindruck erhält, er befinde sich im Betonbauch der Bestie. Die durchgehende Verwendung von dunklem Metall in den oberirdischen Teilen und die rippenartigen Betonpfeiler im Untergeschoß legen eine eindeutige Hierarchie der Räume und Formen fest, während gleichzeitig die Erkennbarkeit und die funktionale Klarheit des Bahnhofs betont werden.

Obwohl der Bahnhof Stadelhofen den Eindruck erweckt, um eine Art ›Dinosauriermetapher‹ herum konzipiert zu sein, ist die zugrundeliegende Idee von Calatravas Entwurf wesentlich komplexer – oder gänzlich andersartig. »Tatsächlich habe ich eine – wie ich es nenne – ›Dialektik der Transgression‹

> Stadelhofen Railway Station, Zurich, Switzerland

on a large scale in the kind of innovative design for which he has become famous.

The curved 40 by 240 meter site required construction during the continued operation of the commuter train line, and was modified to include a large shopping area below ground. The whole has an organic unity, which the circumstances could not have simplified. Like an extravagant flying dinosaur that has come to nest against this hillside, the structure is articulated by a pattern of repeating elements, with enormous anthropomorphic gates leading to the underground shopping mall, where one quickly gets the impression of being in the concrete belly of the beast. There is a continuity in the dark metal above ground and the rib-like concrete below, which establishes a clear hierarchy of spaces and forms, all of this while placing an obvious emphasis on the legibility and functional clarity of the station.

Though it may be that the whole of Stadelhofen Railway Station gives the impression of being conceived around a kind of dinosaur metaphor, the substance of Calatrava's design is more complex, or perhaps different. "In reality, what I have attempted is what I would call a dialectic of transgression, which is based on the vocabulary of structural forces. In Stadelhofen, for example, there are a series of inclined columns. Though this appears to be an esthetic decision, it is in fact related to the necessity of holding up the structure. Naturally there were various solutions for this type of support. They could have been simple cylinders, for example, but I chose to articulate them in the shape of a hand. This is where the question of metaphors becomes interesting. How better to express the function of the columns than to invest them with the sense of the physical gesture of carrying?"[9]

Though Santiago Calatrava's name is often cited with reference to bridges, he is also a recognized specialist in railroad stations, currently working for example on large structures in Lisbon and Liège. One of the buildings that contributed most to his reputation, however, was the Lyon-Satolas TGV terminal

auparavant. De petits espaces verts, comme le voile de verdure suspendu au-dessus du niveau supérieur, ont été créés.» Concrètement, en s'approchant de la gare lorsqu'il vient de la ville, le visiteur se trouve d'abord face au pavillon traditionnel de l'ancienne gare avant d'entrer ou de descendre dans les espaces conçus par Calatrava. «Il était évident dès le départ,» poursuit l'architecte «que le respect témoigné en Suisse aux constructions de plus de cent ans éliminait toute tentative de démolir ou de modifier substantiellement les anciennes installations. Je n'ai pas pour autant jugé cette contrainte illogique, car elle correspond à une lecture de la ville qui est restée intacte.»[8] Une fois ce pavillon traversé, le voyageur pénètre dans un monde très différent qui semble plus proche de l'imaginaire de Gaudí que de celui des paisibles Zurichois. Si Calatrava fait remarquer que Zurich possède une sorte de tradition d'architecture radicale avec les réalisations d'architectes comme Marcel Breuer, il est certain, par ailleurs, que cette gare lui a donné la première grande occasion de mettre en œuvre le type de conception innovante qui allait le rendre célèbre.

Sur ce site en courbe de 40 x 240 m, les travaux de construction se sont déroulés sans gêner le trafic des trains de banlieue. L'opération fut modifiée à un certain moment par l'inclusion en sous-sol d'un centre commercial. L'ensemble présente une unité organique malgré des contraintes qui n'ont pas dû simplifier les travaux. Tel un extravagant dinosaure volant venu se nicher au flanc de la colline, la structure s'articule en éléments répétitifs, interrompus par d'énormes portes zoomorphiques qui mènent au centre commercial souterrain, où l'on a très vite l'impression de se retrouver dans le ventre de la bête. Une continuité se perçoit entre le métal sombre utilisé à l'air libre et les côtes en béton du sous-sol qui déterminent une hiérarchie lisible d'espaces et de formes, le tout mettant en valeur la lisibilité et la clarté fonctionnelle de la gare.

Si l'ensemble de Stadelhofen donne peut-être l'impression

angestrebt, die auf der Formensprache struktureller Kräfte basiert. Der Bahnhof Stadelhofen beispielsweise verfügt über eine Reihe geneigter Pfeiler. Obwohl es sich dabei auf den ersten Blick um eine rein ästhetische Maßnahme handelt, geht es bei diesen Pfeilern tatsächlich um die Notwendigkeit, die Konstruktion zu tragen. Natürlich gibt es genügend andere Lösungen für diese Art von Stützpfeilern; ich hätte sie beispielsweise als einfache Zylinder ausführen können, aber ich entschied mich dafür, sie wie eine menschliche Hand zu gestalten. Und hier erhält die Frage nach der Metapher eine interessante Wendung: Wie könnte man die Funktion der Pfeiler wohl besser ausdrücken als durch eine Gestaltung, die an die natürliche Geste des Tragens erinnert?«[9]

Obwohl Santiago Calatravas Name häufig im Zusammenhang mit modernen Brücken fällt, ist er auch ein anerkannter Spezialist für Bahnhöfe, wie seine derzeitigen Bahnhofsprojekte in Lissabon und Lüttich zeigen. Unter den Gebäuden, die am stärksten zu seinem Ruf beitrugen, ist u.a. der TGV-Bahnhof Lyon-Satolas (1989–94). Dieser 5 600 m² große Bahnhof am Flughafen Satolas gehört zu einer neuen Generation von Bahnhöfen, die eigens für Frankreichs wachsendes Netz von Hochgeschwindigkeitszügen (TGV) konzipiert wurden. Durch die Kombination von Bahn, Flugzeug und öffentlichem Nahverkehr an einem Ort entstand ein effizienter Verkehrsknotenpunkt. Der Passagierterminal wurde am 7. Juli 1994 eröffnet. Er ist 120 Meter lang, 100 Meter breit und 40 Meter hoch und ruht auf einem zentralen, 1300 Tonnen schweren Stahlgerüst. Der Bahnhof erinnert mit seiner Form eines zum Flug ansetzenden Vogels an Eero Saarinens TWA–Terminal am John F. Kennedy Airport (1956–62), ist jedoch noch expressiver als sein amerikanischer Vorläufer. Der Grundriß des Komplexes mit seiner Verbindung zum Flughafen erinnert an einen Stachelrochen. Unterhalb des Hauptgebäudes verlaufen sechs Gleise, auf denen die Züge an 500 Meter langen, überdachten Bahnsteigen halten. Die beiden mittleren Gleise für Hochgeschwindigkeitszüge mit Spitzengeschwindigkeiten von über 300 Kilometern in der Stunde sind von einer Betonhulle umgeben, deren Konstruktion eine sorgfältige Berechnung der Druckwelle erforderte, die der TGV erzeugt. Die Gesamtkosten von über 600 Millionen Francs teilten sich die Französische Staatsbahn (SNCF), die Regionalverwaltung Rhône–Alpes und das Département Rhône.

Wenn man ihn zum Bild des prähistorischen Vogels befragt, antwortet Calatrava auf seine charakteristische indirekte und dennoch informative Weise: »Ich bin nur ein Architekt und kein Künstler oder jemand, der eine Revolution auslösen möchte. Interessanterweise verglich Victor Hugo in seinem Roman *Der Glöckner von Notre Dame* die Kathedrale mit einem urzeitlichen Monster. Obwohl er möglicherweise hervorragende Kenntnisse der Architektur besaß und sich dessen, was er schrieb, durchaus bewußt war, ließ er es sich nicht nehmen, eine so ungewöhnliche Metapher bei der Beschreibung von Notre Dame zu verwenden. Ich suche wirklich nicht nach Metaphern. Und ich habe auch nicht an einen Vogel gedacht, sondern vielmehr an die Vorstudien, die ich manchmal –

> Lyon-Satolas Airport Railway Station, Lyon, France

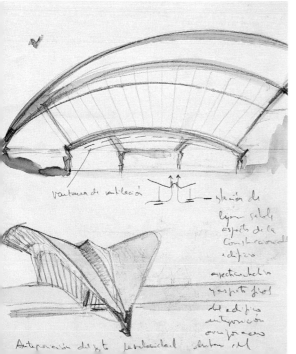

(1989–94). This 5600 square meter station located at the Satolas airport is one of a new generation of rail facilities designed to service France's growing network of high-speed trains (TGV). The juxtaposition of rail, air and local transport facilities at a single location makes for a particularly efficient system. 120 meters long, 100 meters wide, and 40 meters high, the passenger terminal, which opened on July 7, 1994, is based on a central steel element weighing 1300 tons. Calatrava's station seems to echo Eero Saarinen's TWA Terminal at Kennedy Airport (1957–62) in its suggestion of a bird in flight, but it is more exuberant than its American ancestor. The plan of the complex, with its link to the airport, also resembles a manta ray. A total of six train lines run below the main building, and stop at a 500 meter long covered platform also designed by Calatrava. The middle tracks, intended for through trains moving at over 300 kilometers per hour, are enclosed in a concrete shell, a system that required careful calculation of the "shock waves" surrounding the TGV. Shared by the French national rail company (SNCF), the Rhone-Alpes region and the Rhone Department, the total cost of this facility exceeded 600 million francs.

When asked about the image of a prehistoric bird, Calatrava responds in a typically oblique yet informative manner: "I am merely an architect," he says, "not an artist or someone who is seeking to foment a revolution. It might be interesting to note that Victor Hugo in his novel *Notre-Dame de Paris* compares the cathedral to a prehistoric monster. Despite the fact that he may have had an excellent knowledge of architecture, and that he was a very conscientious writer, he used such an unexpected metaphor in describing Notre-Dame Cathedral. I honestly am not looking for metaphors. I never thought of a bird, but more of the research that I am sometimes pretentious enough to call sculpture."[10] Indeed, both the drawings and the sculpture by Calatrava that are most closely related to Satolas seem to find their origin not in the metaphor of a bird, but in a study of the eye and the eyelid,

d'avoir été inspiré par une métaphore d'animal préhistorique, la substance des plans de Calatrava n'en est pas moins plus complexe, ou peut-être différente. «En réalité, j'ai tenté ce que je pourrais appeler une dialectique de transgression, qui repose sur le vocabulaire des forces structurelles. À Stadelhofen, par exemple, se trouve une série de colonnes inclinées. Bien qu'elles puissent sembler relever d'une décision esthétique, elles sont en fait déterminées par la nécessité de soutenir la structure. Naturellement, plusieurs solutions auraient pu remplir le même office. J'aurais pu, par exemple, dessiner de simples cylindres, mais j'ai choisi une articulation en forme de main. C'est ici que le problème de la métaphore devient intéressant. Comment mieux exprimer la fonction des colonnes qu'en les investissant du sens du geste physique de porter?»[9]

Si le nom de Calatrava est souvent cité dès que l'on parle de ponts, il est également l'un des spécialistes reconnus des gares de chemin de fer. Il travaille, par exemple, actuellement sur d'importantes installations nouvelles à Lisbonne et à Liège. L'une des réalisations qui a le plus contribué à sa notoriété reste la gare de TGV de Lyon-Satolas (1989–94). Cette construction de 5 600 m² située sur l'aéroport de Satolas appartient à cette nouvelle génération d'installations conçues pour accompagner le développement du réseau de trains à grande vitesse français. La juxtaposition du rail, de l'avion et des transports locaux sur un seul site est un système particulièrement efficace. Mesurant 120 m de long, 100 de large et 40 de haut, la gare des voyageurs, inaugurée le 7 juillet 1994, repose sur un élément central en acier pesant 1 300 tonnes. Dans sa suggestion d'oiseau en vol, elle semble faire écho au terminal construit par Eero Saarinen à Kennedy Airport (1957–62), tout en étant plus exubérante que son ancêtre américaine. Le plan de cet ensemble et de sa liaison à l'aéroport fait également penser à une raie manta. Six voies courent sous le bâtiment principal et les trains s'arrêtent devant des quais de 500 m de long, également dessinés par l'architecte.

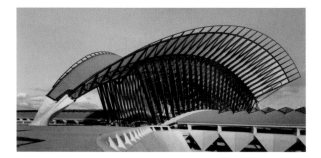

vielleicht etwas vermessen – als Skulpturen bezeichne.«[10] Tatsächlich scheinen sowohl Calatravas Zeichnungen als auch seine Skulpturen, die deutliche Bezüge zum Bahnhof Lyon-Satolas aufweisen, ihren Ursprung nicht in der Metapher eines Vogels zu haben, sondern in seiner Studie des Auges und Augenlids – ein häufig wiederkehrendes Thema in seinen Werken. »Das Auge«, so Calatrava, »ist das wahre Werkzeug des Architekten, und dieser Gedanke geht bis auf die Babylonier zurück.«

Die geschwungene Front des Bahnhofs Lyon-Satolas, die tief ins Erdreich zu dringen scheint, wurde mit einem Vogelschnabel verglichen, aber auch hier ging Calatrava von einer völlig anderen Vorstellung aus. »Der ›Schnabel‹ war das Ergebnis umfangreicher Berechnungen der Kräfte, die auf die Konstruktion einwirken. Gleichzeitig dient er als Sammelpunkt für das Regenwasser. Ich bemühte mich, die Masse dieses Punktes auf ein Minimum zu reduzieren, ohne dabei auch nur einen Gedanken auf ein anthropomorphes Design zu verwenden«, erklärt er. Allerdings bekennt Calatrava, daß es sich bei der Orientierung an seinen eigenen Skulpturen als Ausgangspunkt für den Entwurf um eine ebenso rein ästhetische Frage gehandelt hat, wie es bei einem bewußt gewählten anthropomorphen Konzept der Fall gewesen wäre. Er fügt hinzu: »Wenn Sie so wollen, nennen Sie es irrational. Aber ich meine, daß es keinen Weg gibt, dem man folgen kann. Ich möchte sein wie ein Schiff im Meer. Es läßt einen Kielsog zurück, aber vor dem Bug ist keine Welle zu sehen.«[11]

Ein kürzlich entstandener Entwurf für den TGV-Bahnhof in Lüttich läßt einige Veränderungen in Calatravas Denkmodell erkennen und veranschaulicht die Unterschiede zwischen der ausgeprägten Schlichtheit seiner Brücken und dem komplexeren und offensichtlich ›anthropomorphen‹ Charakter seiner größeren Bauwerke. »Bei den Brücken liegt es in der Natur der Sache, daß sie einen äußerst sparsamen Umgang mit den finanziellen Mitteln erfordern. Wir haben eine Brückentafel, den Bogen, der sie stützt, und die Fundamente, die jeweils etwa ein Drittel der Kosten ausmachen. Angesichts der einfachen Funktion einer Brücke bleibt nur wenig Spielraum für zusätzliche Eingriffe. Dagegen hat man bei einem Bahnhof mindestens sechzehn Ansatzpunkte für individuelle Entscheidungen, die Einfluß auf die ästhetische Gestaltung ausüben – von der Wahl der Metallfensterrahmen bis hin zum Beleuchtungssystem. Es ist den Fähigkeiten des Entwerfenden überlassen, die von ihm angestrebten Ergebnisse im Rahmen der finanziellen Bedingungen eines solchen Projekts zu erzielen.« Ungeachtet dieser grundlegend andersartigen Situation wird deutlich, daß Calatravas Vorliebe für ›Transgressionen‹, für Verstöße gegen traditionelle Vorstellungen, ihn zum Entwurf ungewöhnlicher Brücken und unkonventioneller Bahnhöfe inspiriert. »Nehmen Sie beispielsweise den neuen TGV-Bahnhof in Lüttich«, fährt er fort. »Wir haben die Fassade völlig neu gestaltet; eigentlich gibt es gar keine Fassade. Das ist meines Erachtens eine einschneidende Transgression. Statt einer Fassade wird dieser Bahnhof nur große Öffnungen haben, die durch Metallschutzdächer akzentuiert werden, die in den Bahnhofsvorplatz hineinragen.« Laut Calatrava hat diese Entscheidung tiefgreifende

< Lyon-Satolas Airport Railway Station, Lyon, France
> The Bird

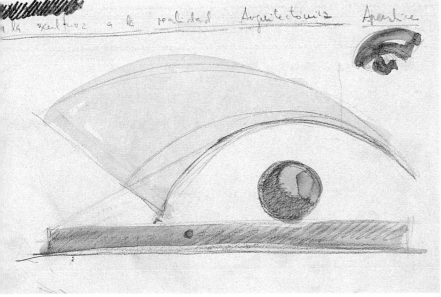

a recurring theme in his work. "The eye," says Calatrava, "is the real tool of the architect, and that is an idea that goes back to the Babylonians."

The swooping front of the Satolas Station, which runs right into the earth, has been compared to the beak of the bird, but Calatrava once again seems to have had an entirely different idea in mind. "The 'beak' was formed as the result of complex calculations of the forces playing on the structure. It also happens to be the assembly point for the water run-off pipes. Naturally, I did my best to minimize the mass of that point, without any thought of an anthropomorphic design," he says. Admitting that the use of his own sculptures as a starting point for the design represents as much of an esthetic choice as would a consciously anthropomorphic concept, Calatrava says, "Call it irrational if you will, but I would say that there is no path to follow. I want to be like a boat in the sea. Behind it there is a trail, but in front there is no path."[11]

A more recent design by Calatrava for the Liège TGV Station shows some changes in his thinking, and illustrates reasons for the differences between the pared down simplicity of his bridges and the more complex and apparently "anthropomorphic" feeling of his larger buildings. "Bridges by their very nature necessitate a strict economy of means. You have the bridge surface, the arc that supports it, and the foundations, with each representing about one third of the cost. Given the simplicity of the function of a bridge, there is only limited margin for intervention. On the other hand, in a railway station, there are at least sixteen types of decision which can have an esthetic impact, from the choice of metal window frames to the lighting design and so on. It is up to the skills of the designer to obtain the result he has imagined within the economic constraints of such a project." Despite this fundamentally different situation, it can readily be seen that Calatrava's taste for "transgression" or innovation pushes him equally to design unusual bridges and unexpected stations.

Les voies centrales, conçues pour des trains traversant la gare à plus de 300 km/h, sont incluses dans une coquille de béton et ont nécessité des calculs poussés sur l'onde de choc que déplace le TGV. Financé par la SNCF, la Région Rhône-Alpes et le département du Rhône, le coût total de cet équipement a dépassé 600 millions de francs.

Lorsqu'on l'interroge sur ces images d'oiseaux préhistoriques, Calatrava répond d'une manière typiquement détournée, mais qui n'en est pas moins riche en éléments d'information : «Je suis essentiellement un architecte,» dit-il, «et non pas un artiste ou quelqu'un qui s'efforcerait de fomenter une révolution. Il est intéressant de noter que Victor Hugo compare, dans Notre-Dame de Paris, la cathédrale à un monstre préhistorique. Même s'il avait peut-être une excellente connaissance de l'architecture et était un écrivain très consciencieux, il ne s'est pas privé d'utiliser une métaphore aussi inattendue pour décrire Notre-Dame. Honnêtement, je ne suis pas à la recherche de métaphores. Je n'ai jamais pensé à un oiseau, mais plutôt à une recherche que je qualifie parfois sans trop de modestie de sculpturale.»[10] En fait, les dessins et la sculpture de Calatrava qui se rapprochent le plus de Satolas semblent trouver leur origine non pas dans une métaphore aviaire, mais dans l'étude de l'œil et de la paupière, thème récurrent dans son œuvre. L'œil, dit-il, «est le grand outil de l'architecte, et cette idée remonte aux Babyloniens.»

La partie busquée de la gare de Satolas qui plonge droit dans le sol a été comparée au bec d'un oiseau, mais, là encore, Calatrava semble avoir eu une idée totalement différente en tête. «Le 'bec' est le résultat d'un calcul complexe des forces jouant sur la structure. C'est également le point de confluence des conduits d'évacuation des eaux. Naturellement, je me suis efforcé de minimiser la masse de ce point précis, mais sans aucune pensée zoomorphique,» explique-t-il. Tout en admettant que l'utilisation qu'il fait de ses propres sculptures dans la mise en forme initiale de ses projets puisse être considérée comme un choix

> Lyon-Satolas Airport Railway Station, Lyon, France

"Take the case of the new TGV Station in Liège," he continues. "We reinvented the facade completely. Or rather there is no facade. That in my opinion is a fundamental transgression. In the place of a traditional facade, there will only be large openings signaled by metal awnings overhanging the square in front of the station." As Calatrava points out, this design decision has important consequences for the functional layout of the station. In a more symbolic vein it might be asked how a station with no facade can be identified as such. "The setting is an urban one, and it seemed to me that the first vision that travelers or visitors would have of the station would be important," explains Calatrava. "My solution was twofold. As it is located on a hill, and is approached from above, there is a view on the city and on the layout of the station. The plan thus becomes the real facade. In order to improve the rapport between the city and the station, we proposed to create a square in front of it."[12] It would seem that this strategy of absence or of a kind of minimalism will bring the Liège station closer to the bridges in its concept than some of Santiago Calatrava's earlier buildings. As for his taste for "transgression," it becomes apparent that Calatrava's careful methods imply a respect for the economic and functional conditions of a project, and seek out a specific reasoning within the gamut of available technical possibilities. He is no wild artist, rummaging through dinosaur skeletons for far-fetched ideas. As Nervi asked, "Why do these forms satisfy and move us in the same manner as natural things such as flowers, plants, and landscapes to which we have become accustomed through numberless generations?" Undoubtedly because they spring from the fertile imagination of the architect/engineer, but also because they respect, from the outset, the fundamental forces at play.

REDISCOVERING THE BRIDGE

As Santiago Calatrava says himself, designing a bridge involves a very specific set of issues, not the least of them symbolic. "If you

esthétique autant qu'un concept zoomorphique, il ajoute «Vous pouvez trouver cela irrationnel, mais je voudrais dire qu'il n'y a pas là de piste. Je veux être comme un navire en mer : derrière, le sillage, et rien devant.»[11]

Un projet plus récent de Calatrava pour la gare de TGV de Liège montre une évolution de sa pensée, et illustre certaines raisons des différences entre la forme épurée de ses ponts et l'impression plus complexe et apparemment zoomorphique qui ressort de ses grands bâtiments. «Par leur nature même, les ponts exigent une stricte économie de moyens. Chaque partie – tablier, arche de soutènement et fondations – représente environ un tiers du coût. Étant donnée la simplicité de fonction d'un pont, la marge d'intervention est très limitée. D'un autre côté, vous trouvez dans une gare au moins seize types de décisions, dont chacune exerce un impact esthétique, du choix des cadres métalliques des ouvertures au design de l'éclairage... C'est au talent du concepteur que l'on doit d'arriver à la solution qu'il a imaginé dans le cadre des contraintes économiques d'un tel projet.» Malgré cette problématique fondamentalement différente, on voit que le goût de Calatrava pour la «transgression» ou l'innovation le pousse aussi bien vers la conception de ponts peu ordinaires que de gares surprenantes. «Prenez le cas de la nouvelle gare TGV de Liège,» poursuit-il, «nous avons complètement réinventé la façade. Ou mieux, il n'y a plus de façade, ce qui est, à mon sens, une transgression fondamentale. À la place d'une façade traditionnelle on ne trouvera que de grandes ouvertures signalées par des auvents métalliques surplombant la place sur laquelle donne le bâtiment.» Mais, comme il le fait remarquer, ce choix n'est pas sans importantes conséquences sur l'agencement fonctionnel du lieu. Comment une gare sans façade peut-être identifiée comme telle? «Le site est urbain, et il m'a semblé que la première vision que les voyageurs ou les visiteurs auront de la gare sera importante,» explique Calatrava. «Ma solution est en deux parties. Comme le bâtiment se trouve sur une colline et

Auswirkungen auf den funktionalen Aufbau des Bahnhofs. In symbolischer Hinsicht stellt sich die Frage, wie ein Bahnhof ohne Fassade als solcher erkannt werden soll. »Der Bahnhof liegt in einem städtischen Umfeld, und es erschien mir wichtig, daß Reisende und Besucher beim Anblick des Bahnhofs einen unvergeßlichen Eindruck erhalten«, erläutert Calatrava. »Mein Konzept sieht eine doppelte Lösung vor. Wenn man sich dem an einem Hügel gelegenen Bahnhof von oben nähert, bietet sich dem Betrachter ein Blick über die Stadt und die gesamte Bahnhofsanlage, die somit selbst zur Fassade wird. Um die Beziehungen zwischen der Stadt und dem Bahnhof zu verbessern, entwarfen wir direkt vor dem Bahnhof einen Platz.«[12] Es scheint, daß diese Strategie der fehlenden Fassade oder einer Art Minimalismus den Bahnhof Lüttich bezüglich seines Konzepts in größere Nähe zu Calatravas Brücken treten läßt als einige seiner früheren Bauwerke. Wie bei seiner Vorliebe für »Transgressionen« ist auch hier Calatravas Respekt vor den wirtschaftlichen und funktionalen Bedingungen eines Projekts erkennbar. Calatrava ist kein wilder Künstler, der sich auf der Suche nach Ideen durch Dinosaurierskelette wühlt. Auf Nervis Frage »Warum befriedigen und bewegen uns diese Formen auf ähnliche Weise wie natürliche Dinge – Blumen, Pflanzen und Landschaften, an die wir uns bereits vor zahllosen Generationen gewöhnt haben?« muß die Antwort lauten: Zweifellos deshalb, weil sie der fruchtbaren Phantasie des Architekten/Bauingenieurs entspringen, aber auch deshalb, weil sie von Beginn an das Spiel der fundamentalen Kräfte respektieren.

DIE WIEDERENTDECKUNG DER BRÜCKE

Wie Santiago Calatrava selbst erläutert, spielen beim Entwurf von Brücken viele verschiedene Faktoren eine Rolle – nicht zuletzt der der Symbolik. »Wenn man die Geschichte der Brücken im 19. und 20. Jahrhundert betrachtet«, erläutert er, »fällt auf, daß es sich bei vielen um ganz besondere und signifikante Konstruktionen handelt. Sie besaßen Natursteinverkleidungen, Löwenskulpturen oder Geländer und Brüstungen. Bei der Pont Alexandre III in Paris werden die Lampen sogar von Engeln getragen. Diese Einstellung zum Brückenbau änderte sich nach dem Zweiten Weltkrieg, als in ganz Europa Hunderte von Brücken in kürzester Zeit wieder aufgebaut werden mußten. Aus purer Notwendigkeit entwickelte sich so eine Schule des rein funktionalen Brückenbaus. Nur eine schlichte und allem voran preiswerte Brücke war eine gute Brücke.«

Calatrava vertritt die Ansicht, daß diese Schule des funktionalistischen Brückenbaus der Nachkriegszeit mit ihrer Zweckdienlichkeit längst überholt ist. »Wir müssen heute das Potential der Brücken wiedererkennen«, erklärt er und führt verschiedene europäische Städte wie Florenz, Venedig und Paris als Beispiele an, um die Tatsache zu unterstreichen, daß die Brücken der vergangenen Jahrhunderte wegen ihrer Zweckmäßigkeit, aber auch wegen ihrer Beständigkeit eine Schlüsselrolle für den Gesamteindruck dieser Städte spielten. Um seine These zu untermauern, erklärt Calatrava sogar, daß der Bau einer Brücke ein folgenreicherer kultureller Akt sein kann als der Bau eines neuen

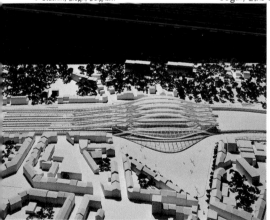

> Station, Liège, Belgium

look back over the history of nineteenth and twentieth century bridges," says Calatrava, "many are very special and significant structures. They were given stone cladding, sculpted lions or railings, even angels holding the lamps as is the case on the Alexander III bridge in Paris. This attitude disappeared as a result of World War II," he continues. "Hundreds of bridges all over Europe had to be rebuilt quickly. It was out of necessity that a school of purely functionalist bridge design sprang up. A good bridge was a simple one, and above all a cheap one." Calatrava obviously feels that this functionalist school of bridge design has far outlived its post-War usefulness. "Today, we have to rediscover the potential of bridges," he declares. He cites the examples of European cities such as Florence, Venice or Paris to highlight the fact that through their usefulness, but also their permanence, bridges of the past have had a key role in forming impressions of the cities themselves. To make his point Santiago Calatrava goes so far as to say that building a bridge can be a more potent cultural gesture than creating a new museum. "The bridge is more efficient," he says, "because it is available to everyone. Even an illiterate person can enjoy a bridge. A single gesture transforms nature and gives it order. You can't get any more efficient than that," he concludes.[13]

The success of Calatrava's own efforts to give a new meaning to bridges might best be summed up by the example of the Alamillo Bridge and La Cartuja Viaduct (Seville, 1987–92). Standing out at one of the entries to Expo '92, the spectacular 142 meter high pylon is inclined at a 58 degree angle (the same as that of the Great Pyramid of Cheops near Cairo), making it visible from much of the old city of Seville. Supported by thirteen pairs of cables, the Alamillo Bridge has a 200 meter span, and runs over the Meandro San Jeronimo, an all but stagnant branch of the Guadalquivir River. It is supported by thirteen pairs of stay cables, but above all, the "weight of the concrete-filled pylon is sufficient to counterbalance the deck, therefore back stays

s'approche par le haut, on dispose d'une vue sur la ville et l'agencement de la gare. Le plan devient ainsi la vraie façade. Par ailleurs, pour améliorer le rapport entre la ville et la gare, nous avons proposé de créer une place devant celle-ci.»[12] On peut penser que cette stratégie d'absence, ou d'une sorte de minimalisme, rapproche plus le concept de cette gare des ponts que de certains bâtiments antérieurs de Calatrava. De même que pour son goût de la «transgression», il devient de plus en plus apparent que les approches calculées de l'architecte impliquent un respect des conditions économiques et de la fonctionnalité du projet, et cherchent à favoriser une réflexion spécifique dans la gamme des possibilités techniques offertes. Ce n'est certainement pas un artiste en liberté, fouillant dans les squelettes de dinosaures pour trouver quelque concept extrémiste. Comme se le demande Nervi : «Pourquoi ces formes nous satisfont-elles et nous émeuvent-elles de la même manière que les objets de la nature, comme les paysages, les plantes et les fleurs auxquels nous sommes habitués depuis des générations?» Sans aucun doute parce qu'elles naissent de l'imagination fertile de l'architecte-ingénieur, mais également parce qu'elles respectent dès l'origine les forces fondamentales en jeu.

REDÉCOUVRIR LE PONT

Comme le dit Santiago Calatrava lui-même, concevoir un pont implique des enjeux très spécifiques, dont les plus symboliques ne sont pas les moins importants. «Si vous vous penchez sur l'histoire des ponts aux XIXᵉ et XXᵉ siècles,» dit-il, «beaucoup d'entre eux constituent des structures très particulières, chargées de sens. On les parait de pierre, de lions sculptés, de moulures, et même d'angelots tenant des lampadaires, comme dans le cas du pont Alexandre III à Paris. Cette attitude disparaît après la Seconde Guerre mondiale. Il fallait alors reconstruire très rapidement des centaines d'ouvrages dans toute l'Europe, et c'est de cette nécessité qu'a

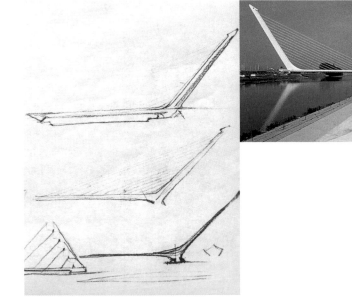

Museums. »Die Brücke ist effizienter«, meint er, »da sie jedermann zugänglich ist. Eine Brücke ist auch Menschen zugänglich, die sich nicht für Kunst interessieren. Eine einzige Geste verwandelt die Natur und gibt ihr eine Ordnung. Noch effizienter geht es einfach nicht.«.

Der Erfolg von Calatravas eigenen Bemühungen, Brücken eine neue Bedeutung zu verleihen, läßt sich am besten an der Alamillo-Brücke und dem La Cartuja-Viadukt (Sevilla, 1987–92) ablesen. Als einer der herausragenden Beiträge zur Expo '92 ist dieser aufsehenerregende, 142 Meter hohe Pylon, dessen Neigungswinkel von 58 Grad dem der Cheopspyramide entspricht, von fast allen Punkten der Altstadt Sevillas aus sichtbar. Die von 13 Kabelpaaren getragene Brücke besitzt eine Spannweite von 200 Metern und erstreckt sich über den Meandro San Jeronimo, einen Nebenfluß des Guadalquivir. Ungeachtet der Unterstützung durch die 13 Kabelpaare ist »das Gewicht des mit Beton gefüllten Stahlpylons ausreichend, um als Gegengewicht für die Brückentafel zu dienen, wodurch Verstrebungen überflüssig werden.«[14] Obwohl Calatrava ursprünglich eine zweite Brücke mit einem spiegelbildlich geneigten Pylon zur Überquerung des in der Nähe fließenden Guadalquivir plante, entschied sich der Auftraggeber, die Regierung der Provinz Andalusien, aus finanziellen Gründen für nur eine Brücke und das 500 Meter lange Puenta de la Cartuja-Viadukt.

Neben den Skizzenbüchern, die seine Überlegungen beim Entwurf der innovativen Form des Alamillo-Pylons veranschaulichen, diente Calatrava seine 1986 entworfene Skulptur »Running Torso« als wichtige Inspirationsquelle – eine Skulptur, »deren schräg übereinander gestapelte Marmorwürfel durch unter Spannung stehende Drahtseile im Gleichgewicht gehalten werden.«[15] Tatsächlich zeigen viele Zeichnungen Calatravas, die die Wände seines Hauses in Zürich schmücken, Torsi in Bewegung. Auch »Running Torso« ist – wie der Name schon sagt – von der Spannung und den Kräften eines nach vorne strebenden Körpers inspiriert. Obwohl Calatravas Umsetzung dieser Analyse sehr persönlich ausfällt, enthält das Ergebnis Aspekte des von Nervi beschworenen »wahrhaften Stils«.

Überraschenderweise war das Alamillo-Projekt vor seiner Errichtung heftig umstritten. Calatrava erzählt: »Eine Reihe von Ingenieuren versuchte den Beweis anzutreten, daß die Konstruktion nicht halten oder viel teurer ausfallen würde als erwartet. Sie ließen sogar die Berechnungen noch einmal überprüfen.« Obwohl Neid und Mißgunst unter Kollegen in Architektur und Ingenieurbau ebenso häufig vorkommen wie in anderen Berufssparten, gelangen sie nur selten an die Öffentlichkeit. Calatrava bleibt angesichts solcher Schwierigkeiten gelassen. »Ich bin mir durchaus bewußt, daß viele meiner Kollegen unter diesem Phänomen stärker zu leiden haben als ich, da sie noch unkonventioneller sind.«[16]

An dieser Stelle sollte darauf hingewiesen werden, daß die Alamillo-Brücke trotz der Kontroverse, die sie ausgelöst hat, auch andere Architekten zur Anwendung eines geneigten Brückenpylons

< Alamillo Bridge, Seville, Spain
> Orleans Bridge over Loire, Orleans, France

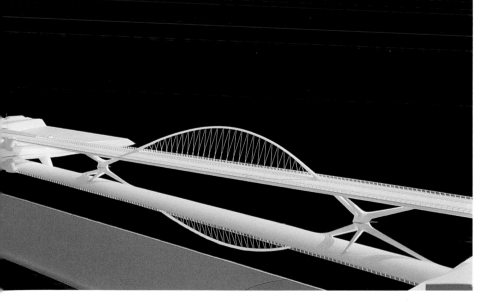

are not required."[14] Although Calatrava had originally imagined a second bridge, inclined in the opposite direction, like a mirror image of the first one, to cross the nearby Gaudalquivir, budgetary considerations made the client, the Junta of Andalucia, opt for only one span together with the 500 meter long Puente de la Cartuja Viaduct.

Aside from his own copiously illustrated notebooks, which make clear the thinking that went into creating the innovative form of the Alamillo pylon, Calatrava here called quite directly on the inspiration provided by "Running Torso," a sculpture he created in 1986, "in which inclined stacked marble cubes are balanced by a tensioned wire."[15] Indeed, many of the drawings that Calatrava hangs on the walls of his Zurich home depict figures in motion. "Running Torso" is clearly inspired, as its title implies, by the tension and forces of a body moving forward. Although the specific use that Calatrava makes of this analysis is very personal, the result does retain something of the "truthful style" evoked by Nervi.

Surprisingly, the Alamillo project was severely contested before its construction. As Calatrava says, "A number of engineers tried to prove that it would not hold up, or that it would be much more costly than expected. They even commissioned someone to redo the calculations," he says. Although professional jealousy is as common in architecture and engineering as in other areas, it does not often become a matter of public knowledge. Calatrava remains philosophical about such difficulties. "I am fully aware," he says, "that many of my colleagues suffer more from this kind of thing than I do because they are even more unconventional."[16]

It should be noted that the Alamillo Bridge seems, despite its controversial aspects, to have already inspired other significant uses of the concept of the inclined pylon. The Dutch architect Ben van Berkel, for example, who spent some time working with Calatrava, recently completed the Erasmus Bridge in Rotterdam (1993–96). Its powerful shape now marks the urban landscape

surgi une école du pont purement fonctionnel.
Un bon pont était un pont tout simple, et surtout bon marché.» Calatrava estime à l'évidence que cette école fonctionnaliste a perdu depuis longtemps l'utilité qui l'avait justifiée après-guerre. «Aujourd'hui, nous devons redécouvrir le potentiel des ponts,» déclare-t-il, et il cite les exemples de villes comme Florence, Venise ou Paris pour souligner qu'à travers leur fonction, mais aussi leur permanence, les ouvrages d'art du passé ont joué un rôle majeur dans l'image de ces cités. Pour résumer sa pensée, il va jusqu'à dire que la construction d'un pont peut se révéler un geste culturel encore plus riche que celle d'un nouveau musée. «Le pont est plus efficace, parce qu'il est à la portée de tous. Même un illettré peut aimer un pont. Un simple geste transforme la nature et crée un ordre. Difficile d'être plus efficace,» conclut-il.[13]

Le succès des efforts de Calatrava pour donner un nouveau sens aux structures de franchissement s'illustre particulièrement dans l'exemple du pont de l'Alamillo et du viaduc de La Cartuja (Séville, 1987–92). Se dressant à l'une des entrées d'Expo '92, le spectaculaire pylône de 142 m de haut s'incline selon un angle de 58° (identique à celui de la grande pyramide de Chéops, près du Caire), visible d'une bonne partie du centre ancien de Séville. Le pont, d'une portée totale de 250 m, franchit le Meandro San Jeronimo, un bras parfois très actif du Guadalquivir. Il est soutenu par 13 paires de haubans, mais surtout «le poids du pylône rempli de béton est suffisant pour contrebalancer celui du tablier, éliminant du même coup la nécessité de haubans arrière.»[14] Calatrava avait à l'origine imaginé un second pont incliné dans le sens opposé, reflet en miroir du premier, pour traverser le Guadalquivir, mais des considérations budgétaires ont obligé le maître d'ouvrage, la Junte d'Andalousie, de s'en tenir à un seul franchissement, ainsi qu'au viaduc de la Cartuja de 500 m de long.

En dehors de ses carnets de notes copieusement illustrés qui retracent les réflexions à l'origine de la conception du pylône

> Alamillo Bridge, Seville, Spain

of central Rotterdam. Although its deck is remarkably thin, this bridge makes use of back stays, unlike Calatrava's Seville design. Whatever their technical qualities, bridges such as these clearly satisfy Santiago Calatrava's call for a new approach, symbolizing the modernity of the cities they grace.

Despite the ease with which the uninformed person can indeed appreciate the beauty of a bridge, the method that leads to these forms is naturally quite complex. "It is an intuitive process, which is to say a system that relies on the synthesis of a number of factors," he says. His description of bridge design deserves to be quoted at length: "I believe that first and foremost, the location of a bridge must be considered. On certain sites, for example, you could not employ an arc because it is not feasible to transfer the loads to the shore in an appropriate manner. Then, too, waterborne traffic must be considered. The height of a bridge can be determined by the type of boats that must past beneath it. The choice of materials is also essential; wood, steel or concrete might be used according to the local circumstances and cost factors. These elements and others lead, by a process of elimination, toward certain possible structural solutions. It is then that not only the type of the bridge itself, but also its impact on its environment, begin to give it form. And then, too, that the engineer must make the calculations necessary to be certain that the design he imagines is indeed viable. I create a model that links mathematical science to nature, permitting an understanding of the behavior of nature. We are always confronted with the forces of nature," he concludes.[17]

One of Santiago Calatrava's recently completed bridges, the Campo Volantin Footbridge (Bilbao, Spain, 1990–97) is exemplary in terms of his thoughts on peripheral or industrial urban spaces, as well as a proficient exercise in engineering resulting in an unexpected form. Crossing the Bilbao River in a location intended to link the city center with the run-down commercial area called Urbitarte, it calls on the principle of the inclined arch that

de l'Alamillo, Calatrava s'est ici inspiré assez directement d'un «Torse courant», sculpture de 1986, «dans laquelle des cubes de marbre empilés sont tenus en équilibre par un fil métallique en tension.»[15] En fait, de nombreux dessins accrochés aux murs de la résidence zurichoise de Calatrava représentent des figures en mouvement. Comme son titre l'implique, «Le torse courant» est clairement inspiré de la tension et des forces d'un corps en mouvement. Bien que l'utilisation spécifique de cette analyse par l'architecte soit très personnelle, le résultat n'est pas sans rappeler quelque chose du "style véritable" évoqué par Nervi.

De manière surprenante, le projet de l'Alamillo a été très sérieusement contesté dès avant sa construction. Comme le note Calatrava : «Un certain nombre d'ingénieurs ont essayé de prouver qu'il ne pourrait pas tenir ou serait beaucoup plus coûteux que prévu. Ils chargèrent même un ingénieur de refaire les calculs...» Si la jalousie professionnelle est aussi commune en architecture et en ingénierie que dans d'autres domaines, elle n'est pas très souvent portée sur la place publique. Calatrava reste philosophe face à ce genre de difficultés. «Je suis pleinement conscient, » dit-il, «que beaucoup de mes collègues souffrent plus de ce genre de comportements que moi, parce qu'ils sont encore moins conventionnels.»[16]

Quelle que soit la controverse, il faut noter que le pont de l'Alamillo semble avoir déjà inspiré d'autres applications du concept de pylône incliné. L'architecte néerlandais Ben van Berkel, par exemple, qui a travaillé quelque temps auprès de Calatrava, vient d'achever le pont Érasme (1993–96), dont la forme puissante marque maintenant le centre de Rotterdam. Bien que son tablier soit remarquablement mince, il fait appel à des haubans arrière à la différence du projet de Séville. Quelles que soient leurs qualités techniques, les ponts de ce type répondent à la recherche calatravienne d'une approche nouvelle, symbolique de la modernité des villes qu'elles embellissent.

Si la beauté d'un pont s'impose facilement à une personne

inspirierte. Der niederländische Architekt Ben van Berkel beispielsweise, der eine Zeitlang mit Calatrava zusammenarbeitete, stellte vor kurzem seine Erasmusbrücke in Rotterdam (1993–1996) fertig, deren eindrucksvolle Silhouette Rotterdams Innenstadt prägt. Obwohl die Brückendecke außerordentlich dünn ist, setzte der Architekt, im Gegensatz zu Calatrava, zusätzliche Verstrebungen ein. Konstruktionen wie diese bestätigen – abgesehen von ihrer technischen Qualität – Santiago Calatravas Konzept einer innovativen Brückengestaltung, die die Modernität der jeweiligen Städte symbolisiert.

Auch wenn sich dem zufälligen Betrachter die Schönheit einer solchen Brücke unmittelbar erschließt, sind die Verfahren, die zur Entwicklung dieser Formen führen, sehr komplex. »Es handelt sich um einen intuitiven Vorgang bzw. ein System, das auf der Synthese einer Reihe von Faktoren basiert«, erklärt Calatrava. Seine Beschreibung des Brückenentwurfs verdient es, hier in voller Länge zitiert zu werden: »Ich bin der Ansicht, daß an allererster Stelle der zukünftige Standort einer Brücke berücksichtigt werden muß. Beispielsweise kann man an manchen Orten keinen Bogen einsetzen, da sich der Transport der Lasten zum Baugelände nicht auf vernünftige Weise bewerkstelligen läßt. Außerdem muß man den Schiffsverkehr einberechnen; denn die Höhe der Brücke kann durch die verschiedenen Schiffstypen, die unter der Brücke hindurchfahren müssen, bestimmt werden. Auch der Wahl der Materialien kommt besondere Bedeutung zu – Holz, Stahl oder Beton können, je nach den örtlichen Gegebenheiten und nach Kostenfaktor, Verwendung finden. Diese und andere Kriterien führen mit Hilfe einer negativen Zielanalyse zu bestimmten, baulich durchführbaren Lösungen. Erst dann tragen sowohl der gewählte Brückentypus als auch der Einfluß, den die Brücke auf ihre Umgebung ausüben soll, zur Gestaltung ihrer endgültigen Form bei. An diesem Punkt muß der Bauingenieur auch die notwendigen Berechnungen vornehmen, um sicherzugehen, daß der ihm vorschwebende Entwurf tatsächlich durchführbar ist. Ich schaffe ein Modell, das Mathematik und Natur verbindet und ein Verständnis für das Verhalten der Natur ermöglicht. Denn wir werden ständig mit den Kräften der Natur konfrontiert.«[17]

Zu den kürzlich von Santiago Calatrava fertiggestellten Bauwerken zählt auch die Campo Volantin-Fußgängerbrücke (Bilbao, Spanien, 1990–1997), die nicht nur in bezug auf Calatravas These zu Stadtrand- bzw. Industriegebieten exemplarisch ist, sondern auch eine meisterhafte Übung im Ingenieurbau darstellt, die zu einer unerwarteten Form führt. Die den Fluß Bilbao überquerende Konstruktion verbindet das baufällige Industriegebiet Uribitarte mit der Innenstadt von Bilbao. Auch sie beruht auf dem Prinzip des geneigten Bogens, das Calatrava erstmals 1988 bei einem (nicht realisierten) Projekt für eine neue Seine-Brücke zwischen dem 12. und 13. Arrondissement anwandte, die den Gare de Lyon mit dem Gare d'Austerlitz verbinden sollte. Der geneigte Parabelbogen der Campo Volantin-Fußgängerbrücke mit seiner Spannweite von 75 Metern stützt einen geschwungenen

> Sculpture V, Running Torso
> Bauschänzli Restaurant, Zurich, 1988

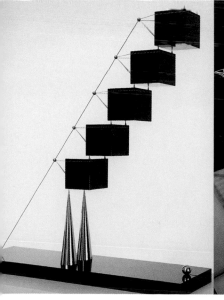
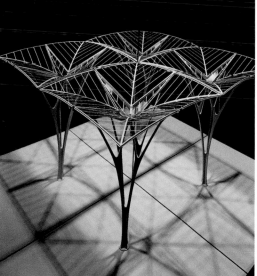

Calatrava first used in an unbuilt 1988 project for a new bridge on the Seine, between the 12th and the 13th arrondissements, linking the Gare de Lyon and the Gare d'Austerlitz. Here, an inclined parabolic arch spanning 71 meters supports a curved walkway, which makes for a visually arresting design. Yet that curve is more than artistic license. As Sergio Polano explains: "The torsion created at the points of suspension of the uprights by the eccentricity of the weight is balanced by the counter-curve of the walkway, thus transferring the load to the concrete foundations," the whole suggesting "a pendulum in suspended motion."[18] As was the case in the Alamillo Bridge, a spectacular lighting system, which accentuates the impact of the bridge into the night, completes this project.

THE LANGUAGE OF TOWERS

It remains to be seen whether Calatrava's theories about the positive impact of a bridge can really change the atmosphere of this area in Bilbao, but it is certain that the city feels that an investment in good architecture and design is worth its while. A new subway line designed by Sir Norman Foster, and the Guggenheim Bilbao Museum recently completed by Frank Gehry, are evidence of the ambitions of this northern Spanish city. Nor is the intervention of Santiago Calatrava limited to the Campo Volantin Footbridge. He has also been asked to expand the airport, adding a new terminal and control tower. The 42 meter high Sondica Airport Control Tower (1993–96), which contains technical facilities, offices and the actual control deck in the form of an inverted, truncated cone, offering a panoramic view to the staff, highlights another area of interest of Calatrava: the tall structure.

The best known of these projects is certainly the Montjuic Communications Tower (Barcelona, 1989–92), which was built at the time of the Olympic Games. Some 130 meters high, with an inclined stem, the tower has been compared to a javelin being

non informée, la méthode qui conduit à ces formes est assez complexe. «C'est un processus intuitif, c'est-à-dire un système qui se nourrit de la synthèse d'un certain nombre de facteurs,» explique l'architecte. Sa description de la conception d'un pont mérite d'être intégralement citée : «Je pense que, d'abord et avant tout, l'emplacement du pont doit être pris en considération. Sur certains sites, par exemple, vous ne pouvez pas faire appel à une arche, parce qu'il est impossible de transférer de façon correcte les charges sur les rives. Le trafic fluvial doit lui aussi être pris en compte, puisque la hauteur d'un pont peut être déterminée par le type de bateaux qui passeront sous son tablier. Le choix des matériaux est également essentiel. Le bois, l'acier ou le béton peuvent être utilisés selon les circonstances locales et les facteurs économiques. Ces éléments, ainsi que d'autres, conduisent à certaines solutions structurelles par un processus d'élimination. C'est alors que non seulement le type de pont lui-même, mais également son impact sur l'environnement commencent à prendre forme. Puis, l'ingénieur doit se livrer aux calculs nécessaires pour être certain que le projet imaginé est bien viable. Je crée également une maquette qui est un lien entre la science mathématique et la nature, et permet une compréhension du comportement de celle-ci. Nous sommes souvent confrontés aux forces de la nature.»[17]

L'un des ponts les plus récemment achevés par Santiago Calatrava, la passerelle de Campo Volantin (Bilbao, Espagne, 1990–97), est à la fois exemplaire de sa réflexion sur les espaces urbains périphériques ou industriels, et d'un exercice d'expertise en ingénierie débouchant sur une forme peu usuelle. Traversant la rivière de Bilbao pour relier le centre ville à une zone commerciale en déshérence appelée Urbitarte, il fait appel au principe de l'arche inclinée, que Calatrava a utilisé pour la première fois dans son projet non réalisé de 1988 pour un pont sur la Seine qui devait relier la gare de Lyon à celle d'Austerlitz. Ici, une arche parabolique inclinée de 71 m de portée soutient une

Fußweg und sorgt so für ein faszinierendes Erscheinungsbild. Dennoch geht es bei dieser Kurvung um mehr als nur um künstlerische Freiheit. Sergio Polano erklärt dazu: »Die Torsion, die an den Aufhängepunkten der Stützen durch die exzentrische Lage des Gewichts entsteht, wird durch die gegenläufige Krümmung des Fußwegs ausgeglichen, wobei die Last zu den Betonfundamenten weitergeleitet wird.« Das Ganze erinnert an »ein Pendel in der Schwebe.«[18] Wie bei der Alamillo-Brücke rundet ein aufsehenerregendes Beleuchtungssystem, das die Brücke auch nachts hell erstrahlen läßt, das Projekt ab.

DIE RHETORIK DER TÜRME

Es bleibt abzuwarten, ob Calatravas Theorien bezüglich der positiven Auswirkungen einer Brücke wirklich die Atmosphäre in diesem Stadtteil Bilbaos verändern können. Eines steht jedoch fest: Die Stadt ist der Ansicht, daß eine Investition in gute Architektur und gutes Design sich durchaus lohnt. Eine neue, von Sir Norman Foster entworfene U-Bahnlinie sowie das Guggenheim Bilbao Museum, das Frank Gehry vor kurzem fertiggestellt hat, zeugen von den architektonischen Ambitionen dieser nordspanischen Stadt. Aber Santiago Calatravas Engagement endet nicht mit dem Entwurf der Campo Volantin-Fußgängerbrücke: Er wurde auch mit den Erweiterungsplänen für den bestehenden Flughafen Sondica beauftragt, die durch ein neues Terminalgebäude und einen neuen Kontrollturm abgerundet werden sollen. Der 42 Meter hohe Tower mit seiner umgekehrten, stumpfen Kegelform beherbergt technische Einrichtungen, Büroräume sowie den eigentlichen Kontrollraum, der den Fluglotsen einen Panoramablick von 360 Grad bietet; er dient als gutes Beispiel für ein weiteres Interessengebiet Calatravas – hohe Bauten.

Das bekannteste dieser Projekte ist sicherlich der Montjuïc-Fernsehturm (Barcelona, 1989–92), der zur Zeit der Olympischen Spiele errichtet wurde. Der 136 Meter hohe Turm mit seinem geneigten Schaft wurde mit einem Speer verglichen; aber auch diesem Bau Calatravas liegt ein ganz unkonventioneller Gedankengang zugrunde. Seine Zeichnungen verdeutlichen, daß der Entwurf auf der Gestalt einer knienden, ein Opfer darbringenden Figur basiert. Darüber hinaus läßt der Grundriß des Turms an freimaurerische Symbole wie etwa den Kompaß denken. Calatrava legt jedoch Wert darauf, daß dieser Eindruck täusche und daß ihm auch hier das menschliche Auge als Inspirationsquelle diente. Natürlich ist auch das Auge ein Freimaurer-Symbol, aber die Idee und das Wesen des Montjuïc-Fernsehturms wurden vielschichtig angelegt – wie auch seine Konstruktionsweise eine überraschend dynamische Form hervorbrachte. Im Katalog zur Ausstellung 1993 heißt es dazu: »Symbolisch bezieht sich der Turm auf die feierlichen Veranstaltungen der Olympischen Spiele. Seine ungewöhnliche Form steht nicht im Widerspruch zu den Gesetzen der Statik, da sich der Massenschwerpunkt an der Basis mit der resultierenden Senkrechten seiner Eigenlast deckt. Der Neigungswinkel des Schafts stimmt mit dem Winkel der Sommersonnenwende in Barcelona überein.

< The Sculpture Bird
> Palacio de las Artes, Valencia, Spain

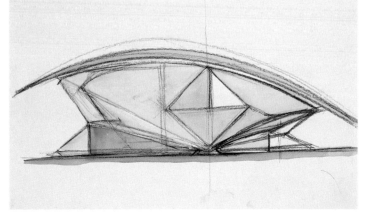

thrown, yet Calatrava's own approach as usual seems to be quite unexpected. His drawings make clear that the vertical design is inspired by the shape of a kneeling human figure making an offering. Similarly, the plan of the tower would seem at first sight to be inspired by Masonic symbols such as the compass. Santiago Calatrava insists that this particular impression is incorrect, and that it is once again the human eye that inspires him. Naturally the eye is also one of the Masonic symbols, but the reasoning and content of the Montjuic Tower are clearly multifaceted, just as its engineering creates a surprisingly dynamic shape. As the catalogue of the 1993 exhibition explains: "Symbolically, the tower refers to the ritual events of the Olympic Games. Its singular form does not contradict the laws of statics, because the center of gravity at the base coincides with the resulting vertical of its dead load. The inclination of the stem coincides with the angle of the summer solstice in Barcelona, and acts as a sundial as the sun travels across the circular platform at the base of the stairs. These characteristics heighten the existence of the two major avenues in Barcelona, La Meridiana and El Paralelo, denoting the avant-garde vocation of this city and referring to the technical advances of the period."[19]

Another tower designed by Santiago Calatrava will not be built, yet deserves to be mentioned because of its spectacular design, and because it was to be a part of the Planetarium and Museum and Opera that he is still working on for his native Valencia. The tower, for which he won a 1991 competition organized by "the Generalitat Valenciana as part of its City of Science project, aimed at rehabilitating a peripheral zone of east Valencia between the Turia River and the superhighway," was to have been the most visible symbolic element of the complex. As Sergio Polano has written: "Rising from a triangular base with convex sides to a height of 382 meters, the tower stands atop an irregular entrance plaza with a circular central court... glass elevators ascend to the viewing platform located approximately halfway up the tower

passerelle en courbe au dessin surprenant. Cependant, cette courbe est plus qu'un parti pris esthétique. Comme l'explique Sergio Polano : «La torsion créée aux points de suspension des montants par la position excentrée du poids est équilibrée par la contre-courbe de la passerelle, transférant ainsi la charge vers les fondations en béton,» l'ensemble suggérant «un pendule en mouvement suspendu»[18]. Comme dans le cas du pont de l'Alamillo, un spectaculaire système d'éclairage accentue l'impact esthétique du pont en nocturne.

LE LANGAGE DES TOURS

Il reste à vérifier si les théories de Calatrava sur l'impact positif d'un pont réussiront à modifier l'atmosphère de ce quartier de Bilbao, mais il est certain que cette ville croit en l'investissement dans une architecture de qualité. Une nouvelle ligne de métro, conçue par Sir Norman Foster, et le Guggenheim Bilbao Museum, récemment achevé par Frank Gehry, illustrent les ambitions de cette grande cité du nord de l'Espagne. L'intervention de Calatrava ne s'est d'ailleurs pas limitée à la passerelle de Campo Volantin. Il a également été chargé de l'extension de l'aéroport, à savoir la création d'un nouveau terminal et d'une tour de contrôle. La tour de l'aéroport de Sondica de 42 m de haut contient des équipements techniques et des bureaux. La salle de contrôle en forme de cône tronqué inversé offre une vue panoramique et illustre un autre centre d'intérêt de Calatrava : les constructions de grande hauteur. Le plus connu de ses projets dans ce domaine est certainement la tour de communications de Montjuic (Barcelone, 1989–92), élevée lors des Jeux Olympiques. Mesurant quelques 130 m de haut, originale par son corps incliné, elle a pu être comparée à un javelot lancé. Comme toujours, l'approche choisie par Calatrava semble assez inattendue. Ses dessins préparatoires montrent que la forme verticale s'inspire de celle d'une figure humaine agenouillée en position d'offrande. De même, le plan de la tour pourrait sembler venir au départ de

So fungiert der Turm als Sonnenuhr, wenn der Schatten entlang der kreisförmigen Plattform am Fuße der Treppen entlangwandert. Diese Anlage hat eine Parallele in den beiden wichtigsten Straßen von Barcelona, >La Meridiana< und >El Paralelo<, die den avangardistischen Zug der Stadt unterstreichen und auf ihre technischen Errungenschaften verweisen.«[19]

Ein anderer von Santiago Calatrava entworfener Turm wird zwar nicht gebaut, sollte hier aber dennoch erwähnt werden, da es sich um einen besonders spektakulären Entwurf handelt. Das Projekt – ein Fernsehturm – war als Teil einer »Stadt der Wissenschaft« in Calatravas Heimatstadt Valencia mit Planetarium, Museum und Oper geplant, mit der der Architekt sich zur Zeit beschäftigt. 1991 gewann er einen vom »Generalitat Valenciana« ausgelobten Wettbewerb, der »die Sanierung eines am östlichen Stadtrand gelegenen Gebietes [vorsah], das sich zwischen einer Autobahn und dem Fluß Turia befindet«. Calatravas Turm sollte dabei den herausragenden und symbolträchtigsten Teil des gesamten Komplexes bilden. Sergio Polano schrieb dazu: »Der Turm erhebt sich über einem dreieckigen Sockel mit konvexen Seiten bis zu einer Höhe von 382 Metern und überragt einen unregelmäßig geformten Eingangsbereich mit einem kreisförmigen, zentralen Innenhof ... In gläsernen Aufzügen gelangt man zu einer Aussichtsplattform, die sich ungefähr auf der Hälfte des Turms (in 172 Metern Höhe) befindet ... Die drei >Füße<, die den Sockel bilden, zeichnen sich durch einen ungewöhnlichen, tropfenförmigen Grundriß aus (ein spitzwinkliges, gleichschenkliges Dreieck mit halbrundem Abschluß) und sind symmetrisch über ein gleichseitiges Dreieck verteilt, das sich wiederum in einem Kreis mit einem Radius von 41 Metern befindet. Die drei mit Glas und Stahlblech ummantelten Stahlbetonsockel verjüngen sich nach oben, bis sie in 162 Metern Höhe im symmetrischen Zentrum der Konstruktion zusammentreffen und die sternförmige Plattform bilden, die den spindelförmigen Schaft mit den Fernmeldeeinrichtungen trägt.«[20]

ZU BAUENDE WELTEN

Einige der interessantesten Entwürfe Santiago Calatravas – wie der Fernsehturm in Valencia – werden wohl nicht realisiert werden. Das ist nicht ungewöhnlich, insbesondere nicht für einen Architekten, der so aktiv wie Calatrava an Ausschreibungen teilnimmt. Dennoch sind Calatravas ungewöhnliche Entwürfe stärkerer Kritik ausgesetzt als andere. »Wenn ich das Ganze einmal aus meiner Sicht beurteilen soll«, erläutert Calatrava, »muß ich sagen, daß mein Wunsch, über das Erwartete hinauszugehen, dem Auftraggeber immer zusammen mit soliden Erklärungen vorgestellt wird. Hier liegt also nicht das Problem. Dagegen haben einige meiner Projekte in der Bauingenieur– und Architekturwelt regelrechte Skandale ausgelöst. Man erregte sich maßlos und warf mir falsche Berechnungen vor, was nun wirklich nicht der Fall zu sein scheint, wenn man sich einmal meine realisierten Projekte ansieht. Architekten gehören zu den konservativsten Menschen, die es gibt. Es ist zwar richtig, daß meine besten Projekte nicht realisiert wurden, aber ich glaube, daß

(172 meters)...The three 'feet' which constitute the base are distinguished by an unusual teardrop plan (a narrow isosceles triangle with a semicircular base), set symmetrically within an equilateral triangle which in turn is inscribed in a circle with a radius of 41 meters. Built in reinforced concrete and sheathed in glass and sheet steel, the triad of base elements taper off as they rise toward the symmetrical center of the structure, meeting at a height of 162 meters to form the star-shaped platform which supports the fusiform telecommunications spire."[20]

WORLDS WAITING TO BE BUILT

A number of the most interesting projects of Santiago Calatrava, like the Valencia tower, will not be built. This fact is not unusual, especially for architects who participate as actively in competitions as he does. And yet it may be that Calatrava's unexpected designs draw more criticism than others. "If I judge things from my point of view," says Calatrava, "my desire to go beyond what is expected is usually presented to the client with very solid explanations. That is not where problems occur. On the other hand, vis-à-vis the community of engineers or architects, some of my projects have stirred up veritable scandals. Clothes were torn, and they have accused me of mad miscalculations, which does not seem to really be the case if you look at my built work. Architects are some of the most conservative people around. It is true that the best projects I have done have not been built, but I find that such admittedly frustrating situations are a necessary part of innovative research."

The largest and in some ways most controversial of Santiago Calatrava's unbuilt projects is his concept for the New German Parliament or Reichstag (Berlin, Germany, 1992). It should be recalled that the Reichstag, whose construction was decided on March 28, 1871, at the eastern end of the Königsplatz, had more than once caused architectural problems in the past. The original 1871 competition winner, Friedrich Bohnstedt, was set aside in

symboles maçonniques comme le compas. L'architecte soutient que cette impression est incorrecte, et que c'est une fois encore l'œil humain qui l'a inspiré. L'œil, pourrait-on dire, est aussi un symbole maçonnique, mais la conception de la Tour de Montjuic et son contenu sont riches de significations multiples, de même que sa technique de construction qui a généré une forme étonnament dynamique. Comme l'explique le catalogue de l'exposition de 1993 : «Symboliquement, la tour se réfère à l'événement rituel des Jeux Olympiques. Sa forme singulière ne contredit pas les lois de la statique, car le centre de gravité coïncide à la base avec la verticale résultante de son poids mort. L'inclinaison correspond à l'angle du solstice d'été à Barcelone, et le fût agit comme une aiguille de cadran solaire lorsque le soleil donne sur la plate-forme circulaire au pied des escaliers. Ces caractéristiques rappellent l'existence de deux grandes avenues de Barcelone, la Meridiana et El Paralelo, échos de la vocation d'avant-garde de la cité et référence au progrès technique de l'époque.»[19]

Une autre tour de Calatrava mérite d'être mentionnée pour sa conception spectaculaire, même si elle ne sera jamais construite. Elle devait faire partie d'un ensemble comprenant un planétarium, un musée et un opéra, sur lequel l'architecte travaille encore pour sa ville natale de Valence. Cette tour, pour laquelle il a remporté en 1991 un concours organisé par «la Généralité de Valence dans le cadre de son projet de Cité des Sciences destiné à réhabiliter une zone périphérique de l'est de la ville entre le fleuve Turia et une autoroute», aurait dû devenir l'élément symbolique le plus visible de ce complexe. Comme l'a écrit Sergio Polano : «S'élevant à partir d'une base triangulaire, avec des faces convexes, jusqu'à une hauteur de 382 m, elle se dresse au sommet d'une place irrégulière à plateau central circulaire... des ascenseurs de verre montent jusqu'à une plate-forme panoramique située à peu près à mi-hauteur (172 m)... Les trois «pieds» qui forment la base se distinguent par un curieux plan en goutte (un étroit triangle

> Reichstag Conversion Competition, Berlin, Germany

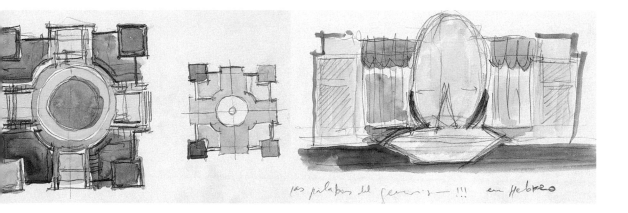

las palabras del genesis — !!! en Hebreo

favor of Paul Wallot a decade later. Wallot himself abandoned the project years before the motto he proposed, "Dem deutschen Volke," was finally engraved on the building. The agony of the Reichstag, from the 1933 fire to the arrival of the Soviets, is of course well known. The renovation and conversion of the Reichstag into the seat of the Bundestag was decided on October 31, 1991, and the competition was announced on June 26, 1992. Three architects – Calatrava, Pi de Bruijn from The Netherlands, and Sir Norman Foster – emerged from this selection process. Foster submitted an unusual large-scale canopy, which would have covered not only the Reichstag itself but also its immediate environment. Calatrava's design, by contrast, sought to give the building a dome once again, to replace the original masonry structure atop the Reichstag demolished after World War II. As Calatrava's drawings and models show, this dome would have been extremely light. As he says, "I made a thin shell from a membrane of light steel profile, which has the effect of being under tension, stressed from within by a cable network. It was my intention to make the lightest, thinnest and most transparent construction possible, executed by the most modern means." Within the dome, petal-like elements would have folded or opened like a flower to bring daylight into the parliamentary chamber below. It is from this point that controversy entered the selection process. Michael Cullen has summed up what occurred as follows: "At the end of April 1993, the three architects were requested to rework their designs, incorporating amended specifications, before June 14th. These new specifications included the use of space in the adjacent Dorotheen block to the east, and the orientation of the assembly hall with the presidential building on the eastern side: both ideas originally conceived by Calatrava. Calatrava was the only one of the three to have further developed his original design; the other two participants came up with radical new solutions. A new session of the jury was not considered necessary. The presentation of the designs on June 17th

isocèle à base semi-circulaire), implanté symétriquement dans un triangle équilatéral qui s'inscrit à son tour dans un cercle de 41 m de rayon. Construits en béton armé et gainés de verre et d'acier, les trois éléments de la base s'amincissent au fur et à mesure qu'ils montent vers le centre symétrique de la structure, se rejoignant à une hauteur de 162 m pour former une plate-forme en étoile qui supporte la flèche en fuseau de la tour de télécommunications.»[20]

CES MONDES QUI ATTENDENT D'ÊTRE CONSTRUITS
Un certain nombre des plus intéressants projets de Santiago Calatrava, comme la tour de Valence, ne seront jamais construits. Ceci n'est pas rare, en particulier pour les architectes qui, comme lui, participent aussi activement aux grands concours. Cependant, il est vraisemblable que ses projets tellement surprenants attirent plus de critiques que d'autres. «De mon côté,» dit-il, «je justifie généralement auprès du client mon désir d'aller au-delà de ce que l'on attend par de très solides explications. Ce n'est pas là que se posent les problèmes. Pour la communauté des ingénieurs ou des architectes, certains de mes projets ont soulevé de véritables scandales. On m'a accusé de grossières erreurs de calcul, ce qui ne semble pas avoir jamais été le cas, si vous considérez ce que j'ai déjà construit. Les architectes sont parmi les gens les plus conservateurs qui soient. Il est vrai que mes meilleurs projets n'ont pas été construits, mais je crois que ce genre de situation, certes frustrant, accompagne nécessairement les recherches les plus innovantes.
Le plus vaste et à certains égards le plus controversé des projets non réalisés de S. Calatrava est sa proposition pour l'installation du Parlement allemand au Reichstag (Berlin, Allemagne, 1992). Ce massif bâtiment, dont la construction avait été décidée le 28 mars 1871 à l'extrémité est de la Königsplatz, a déjà soulevé plus d'une difficulté par le passé. L'architecte vainqueur du concours de 1871, Friedrich Bohnstedt, fut écarté en faveur de Paul Wallot, dix ans

was not public, and no records appear to exist. It was possible to read in the Berlin press on June 19th that a decision had been made in favor of Sir Norman Foster. On June 21st, the Planning Commission of the Council of Elders decided, without obtaining expert advice, to grant the commission to the English architect. On July 1st, with Dr. Rita Süssmuth, the parliamentary president, in the chair, they decided to ask Foster not only to submit more exact plans, but also, in accordance with Calatrava's design, to reconsider the idea of a dome."[21] Foster's revised design was approved by the Bundestag on June 29, 1994. Santiago Calatrava has clearly expressed the opinion that the final design by Foster looks much like his own original concept, a charge that Foster shrugs off as unfounded.

Another interesting unbuilt project by Santiago Calatrava was his competition-winning design for the Cathedral of St. John the Divine (New York, USA, 1991). Built in 1892 and "Gothicized" in 1911, this Manhattan landmark is the largest neo-Gothic church in the world. Adding structural elements with an organic appearance, Calatrava proposed to create a kind of bio-shelter 55 meters above the floor of the church. Gothic church designs were originally inspired by the metaphor of the tree, and Calatrava seizes on this fact to add a garden in the sky that might correspond to the foliage of the metaphorical trees, but which also recalls the story of the Garden of Eden.

Again abundantly illustrated by his drawings and models, the St. John the Divine project highlights Santiago Calatrava's quest for deeper meanings in contemporary architecture. Here, as in most of his major projects, there is a real search not only for functional solutions but also for meaningful references. These references are not always evident, calling as they do on Calatrava's own imagination or his sculptural forms, and yet they do quite obviously retain a truthfulness that explains why he has rapidly become one of the best-known architect-engineers in the world. Transgression is one of Santiago Calatrava's preferred

plus tard. Wallot lui-même abandonna le projet bien des années avant que l'inscription proposée, «Dem deutschen Volk» (Au peuple allemand), ne soit finalement gravée au fronton du bâtiment. L'agonie du Reichstag, de l'incendie de 1933 à l'arrivée de l'Armée Rouge, est bien connue. La rénovation du bâtiment destiné à devenir le nouveau siège du Bundestag a été décidée le 31 octobre 1991, et le concours lancé le 26 juin 1992. Les propositions de Calatrava, du Néerlandais De Bruijn, et de Norman Foster se sont imposées au cours du processus de sélection. Foster avait proposé un immense dais qui aurait recouvert non seulement le bâtiment, mais aussi ses alentours immédiats. Le projet de Calatrava, au contraire, cherchait à redonner au bâtiment un dôme pour remplacer la structure d'origine en maçonnerie, démolie après la Seconde Guerre mondiale. Les dessins et maquettes montrent que cette coupole aurait été extrêmement légère : «J'ai imaginé une coquille très mince constituée à partir d'une membrane de profilés légers en acier, contrainte de l'intérieur par un réseau de câbles. Mon intention était de réaliser la plus légère, la plus mince et la plus transparente des constructions possibles, grâce aux moyens les plus modernes.» À l'intérieur du dôme, des éléments en pétale se seraient ouverts ou refermés comme une fleur pour diffuser la lumière du jour vers la salle du parlement juste en dessous.

Ce dôme allait déclencher la controverse que Michel Cullen az résumée de la façon suivante : «Fin avril 1993, il fut demandé aux trois architectes de retravailler leurs projets pour le 14 juin, en incorporant de nouvelles spécifications qui comprenaient l'utilisation de l'espace dans le bloc Dorotheen à l'est, et l'orientation de la salle du parlement par rapport au bâtiment présidentiel également à l'est, deux idées proposées à l'origine par Calatrava. Celui-ci fut le seul à pousser son projet original, alors que ses concurrents revinrent avec des solutions entièrement différentes. Une nouvelle session du jury ne fut pas jugée nécessaire. La présentation des projets le 17 juin ne fut pas publique, et il semble qu'aucune trace n'en ait été conservée. Le 19 juin, on put lire dans la presse

solche – zugegebenermaßen frustrierenden – Situationen ein notwendiger Bestandteil innovativer Forschung sind.«

Das größte und in mancher Hinsicht umstrittenste Projekt Santiago Calatravas, das nicht realisiert wurde, ist sein Entwurf für den Reichstag in Berlin (1992). An dieser Stelle muß daran erinnert werden, daß der Reichstag, dessen Errichtung am östlichen Ende des Königsplatzes am 28. März 1871 beschlossen wurde, in der Vergangenheit schon mehrfach architektonische Probleme verursacht hatte. Der ursprüngliche Gewinner des Architekturwettbewerbes, Friedrich Bohnstedt, wurde ein Jahrzehnt später zugunsten Paul Wallots übergangen, der wiederum das Projekt nach einiger Zeit aufgab – und zwar Jahre bevor man die von ihm vorgeschlagene Inschrift »Dem Deutschen Volke« schließlich am Gebäude anbrachte. Das Schicksal des Reichstags – vom Brand im Jahre 1933 bis hin zum Einmarsch der sowjetischen Truppen in Berlin – ist allgemein bekannt. Am 31. Oktober 1991 wurde die Sanierung und Umwandlung des Reichstags als Sitz des Bundestags beschlossen, und am 26. Juni 1992 folgte die Ausschreibung, bei der drei Architekten – Calatrava, der Niederländer Pi De Bruijn und Sir Norman Foster – in die engere Wahl kamen. Foster reichte einen Entwurf mit einem ungewöhnlichen, großformatigen Überdach ein, das nicht nur das Reichstagsgebäude, sondern auch seine unmittelbare Umgebung überspannt hätte. Dagegen sah Calatravas Entwurf wieder eine Kuppel für den Reichstag vor, die die nach dem Zweiten Weltkrieg zerstörte, ursprüngliche Konstruktion ersetzen sollte. Wie aus seinen Zeichnungen und Modellen ersichtlich wird, hätte es sich dabei um eine extrem leichte Kuppel gehandelt. Calatrava erklärt dazu: »Ich konstruierte ein dünnes, skelettartiges Rahmenwerk aus einer Dachhaut aus leichtem Profilstahl, die unter Zug stand und von innen von einem Kabelnetz gestützt wurde. Mein Ziel war es, die leichteste, dünnste und transparenteste Konstruktion zu schaffen, die überhaupt möglich war, und diese mit den modernsten Mitteln zu verwirklichen.« Innerhalb der Kuppel hätten sich blütenblattartige Elemente geöffnet, um den darunter liegenden Plenarsaal mit Tageslicht zu versorgen. An diesem Punkt kamen die ersten Meinungsverschiedenheiten über die Vergabe des Auftrags auf. Michael Cullen faßte die dann folgenden Ereignisse zusammen: »Ende April 1993 wurden die drei Architekten aufgefordert, ihre Entwürfe unter Berücksichtigung zusätzlicher Auflagen bis zum 14. Juni noch einmal zu überarbeiten. Diese neuen Auflagen umfaßten auch die Neugestaltung des im Osten angrenzenden Dorotheenblocks sowie die Ausrichtung des Plenarsaals am Sitz des Bundespräsidenten auf der östlichen Seite – zwei von Calatrava bereits vorgesehene Maßnahmen. Überhaupt war Calatrava der einzige der drei Architekten, der seinen Originalentwurf nur überarbeitete; seine Mitbewerber legten völlig neue Konzepte vor. Eine erneute Zusammenkunft der Jury wurde nicht für nötig befunden. Die Präsentation der Entwürfe fand am 17. Juni unter Ausschluß der Öffentlichkeit statt, und es scheinen auch keinerlei Unterlagen zu existieren. Dafür konnte man am 19. Juni in der Berliner Presse lesen,

> Cathedral of St. John the Divine, New York

terms, couched in his own definition of the word, which implies careful study and practical knowledge, applied to the desire to create surprising forms. In his hands bridges and railroad stations have begun to take on a new life, leaving behind the arid functionalism that had its origins in post-War reconstruction. Proceeding as he does from personal sketches and sculpture, Santiago Calatrava is working at a very particular creative edge, where art and architecture, and architecture and engineering, meet. The words of Davioud in 1877 making reference to the accord between architecture and engineering, which he said "will never become real, complete, and fruitful until the day that the engineer, the artist, and the scientist are fused together in the same person," may indeed be descriptive of a talent like that of Santiago Calatrava.

1 Interview with Santiago Calatrava, Paris, November 1995.
2 Giedion, Sigfried: *Space, Time and Architecture*, Harvard University Press, Cambridge, MA, 5th edition, 1976.
3 McQuaid, Matilda: *Santiago Calatrava, Structure and Expression*, The Museum of Modern Art, New York, 1993.
4 Ibid.
5 Interview with Santiago Calatrava, Zurich, June 1997.
6 Ibid.
7 Nervi, Pier Luigi: *Aesthetics and Technology in Building, The Charles Eliot Norton Lectures, 1961–1962*, Harvard University Press, Cambridge, MA, 1965.
8 Interview with Santiago Calatrava, Zurich, June 1997.
9 Ibid.
10 Ibid.
11 Ibid.
12 Ibid.
13 Ibid.
14 Sharp, Dennis (ed.): *Santiago Calatrava*, Architectural Monographs n° 46, Academy Editions, London, 1996.
15 Ibid.
16 Interview with Santiago Calatrava, Zurich, June 1997.
17 Ibid.
18 Polano, Sergio: *Santiago Calatrava, Complete Works*, Gingko, Electa, Milan, 1996.
19 *Santiago Calatrava, 1983–93*, Catalogo de la exposicion antologica en la Lonja de Valencia del 31 de Mayo al 30 de Junio de 1993, El Croquis Editorial, Madrid, 1993
20 Polano, Sergio: *Santiago Calatrava, Complete Works*, Gingko, Electa, Milan, 1996.
21 Cullen, Michael: *Calatrava Berlin, 5 Projects*, Birkhäuser, Berlin, 1994.

1 Entretien avec Santiago Calatrava, Paris, novembre 1995.
2 Giedion, Sigfried, *Space, Time and Architecture*, Harvard University Press, Cambridge, Massachusetts, 5ème édition, 1976.
3 McQuaid, Matilda, *Santiago Calatrava, Structure and Expression*, The Museum of Modern Art, New York, 1993.
4 Ibid.
5 Entretien avec Santiago Calatrava, Zurich, juin 1997.
6 Ibid.
7 Nervi, Pier Luigi, *Aesthetics and Technology in Building, The Charles Eliot Norton Lectures, 1961-62*, Harvard University Press, Cambridge, Massachusetts, 1965.
8 Entretien avec Santiago Calatrava, Zurich, juin 1997.
9 Ibid.
10 Ibid.
11 Ibid.
12 Ibid.
13 Ibid.
14 Sharp, Dennis (éditeur), *Santiago Calatrava*, Architectural Monographs n° 46, Academy Editions, Londres, 1996.
15 Ibid.
16 Entretien avec Santiago Calatrava, Zurich, juin 1997.
17 Ibid.
18 Polano, Sergio, *Santiago Calatrava, Complete Works*, Gingko, Electa, Milan, 1996.
19 *Santiago Calatrava, 1983-93*, Catalogo de la exposicion antologica en la Lonja de Valencia del 31 de Mayo al 30 de Junio de 1993, El Croquis Editorial, Madrid, 1993.
20 Polano, Sergio, *Santiago Calatrava, Complete Works*, Gingko, Electa, Milan, 1996.
21 Cullen, Michael, *Calatrava Berlin, 5 projects*, Birkhäuser, Berlin, 1994.

berlinoise qu'une décision avait été prise en faveur de Norman Foster. Le 21 juin, la commission d'urbanisme du conseil des Anciens décida, sans avoir demandé l'avis d'un expert, de confier la commande à l'architecte britannique. Le 1er juillet, en présence de Rita Süssmuth, présidente du Bundestag, il fut décidé de demander à Foster non seulement de soumettre des plans plus précis, mais également de reconsidérer l'idée d'un dôme, dans l'esprit de la proposition de Calatrava.»[21] Le projet revu par Foster fut approuvé par le Bundestag le 29 juin 1994, et Santiago Calatrava fit clairement savoir que le projet britannique final ressemblait beaucoup au concept qu'il avait proposé, attaque que Foster jugea sans fondement.

Autre projet intéressant, mais non réalisé : la proposition qui remporta le concours pour la Cathédrale de St. John the Divine (New York, 1991). Construit en 1892 et «gothicisé» en 1911, ce célèbre monument de Manhattan est la plus vaste église néogothique du monde. À partir d'éléments structuraux d'apparence organique, Calatrava avait proposé de créer une sorte de bio-refuge à 55 m au-dessus du sol du sanctuaire. Les plans des églises gothiques s'inspiraient à l'origine de la métaphore de l'arbre, et l'architecte s'en était inspiré pour élever un jardin dans le ciel, qui pouvait correspondre au feuillage de l'arbre métaphorique, mais rappelait également le jardin d'Éden.

Une fois encore abondamment explicité par des dessins et des maquettes, ce projet souligne la quête de l'architecte d'une signification plus profonde de l'architecture contemporaine. Ici, comme dans la plupart de ses grands projets, l'on retrouve une recherche non seulement de solutions fonctionnelles, mais également de références porteuses de sens. Celles-ci ne sont pas toujours évidentes, car elles s'appuient sur la propre imagination de Calatrava ou ses sculptures, mais elles manifestent cependant une authenticité qui explique qu'il soit rapidement devenu l'un des architectes-ingénieurs les plus célèbres du monde. La transgression est l'un de ses thèmes préférés, nourrie de sa propre définition du mot qui implique une étude attentive et une connaissance pratique approfondie mises au service du désir de créer des formes surprenantes. Entre ses mains, les ponts et les gares ont commencé à revivre, laissant du même coup de côté l'aride fonctionnalisme de la période de reconstruction d'après–guerre. Progressant à partir de dessins et de sculptures, il œuvre aux marges d'un domaine de la création, où l'art, l'architecture et l'ingénierie se rencontrent. Les mots de Davioud, faisant en 1877 référence à l'accord entre l'architecte et l'ingénieur qui, disait-il : «...ne sera jamais réel, complet et fructueux tant que l'ingénieur, l'artiste et le savant n'auront pas fusionné en une même personne», pourraient être tout simplement la description du talent de Santiago Calatrava.

1 Interview mit Santiago Calatrava, Paris, November 1995.
2 Giedion, Sigfried: *Raum Zeit Architektur.*
Die Entstehung einer neuen Tradition.
Basel/Boston/Wien: Birkhäuser 51996
3 McQuaid, Matilda: *Santiago Calatrava, Structure and Expression*; The Museum of Modern Art,
New York, 1993.
4 ebd.
5 Interview mit Santiago Calatrava, Zürich, Juni 1997.
6 ebd.
7 Nervi, Pier Luigi: *Aesthetics and Technology in Building, The Charles Eliot Norton Lectures, 1961-1962;*
Harvard University Press, Cambridge,
Massachusetts, 1965.
8 Interview mit Santiago Calatrava, Zürich, Juni 1997.
9 ebd.
10 ebd.
11 ebd.
12 ebd.
13 ebd.
14 Sharp, Dennis (ed.): *Santiago Calatrava,*
Architectural Monographs No 46, Academy Editions,
London 1996.
15 ebd.
16 Interview mit Santiago Calatrava, Zürich, Juni 1997.
17 ebd.
18 Polano, Sergio: *Santiago Calatrava, Complete works;*
Gingko, Electa, Mailand 1996.
19 *Santiago Calatrava, 1983-93;* Catalogo de la exposicion antologica en la Lonja de Valencia del 31 de Mayo al 30 de Junio de 1993, El Coquis Editorial,
Madrid 1993.
20 Polano, Sergio: *Santiago Calatrava, Complete works;* Gingko, Electa, Mailand 1996.
21 Cullen, Michael: *Calatrava Berlin, 5 Projekte;* Berlin:
Birkhäuser 1994.

daß die Entscheidung zugunsten Sir Norman Fosters gefallen war. Am 21. Juni beschloß die Planungskommission des Ältestenrats ohne die Mitarbeit weiterer Experten, dem englischen Architekten den Auftrag zu erteilen. Am 1. Juli gelangte die Kommission – unter dem Vorsitz der Bundestagspräsidentin Dr. Rita Süssmuth – zu dem Beschluß, Foster nicht nur um die Einreichung detaillierterer Pläne zu bitten, sondern auch, den Bau einer Kuppel in Erwägung zu ziehen.«[21] Fosters überarbeitete Version wurde am 29. Juni 1994 vom Bundestag angenommen. Santiago Calatrava hat deutlich darauf hingewiesen, daß Fosters endgültiger Entwurf seinem eigenen Originalkonzept frappierend ähnlich sieht – ein Vorwurf, den Foster als unbegründet zurückweist.

Ein weiteres interessantes, nicht realisiertes Projekt Santiago Calatravas ist sein mit dem ersten Preis prämierter Entwurf für die Kirche St. John the Divine in New York (1991). Das 1892 erbaute und 1911 in der Formensprache der Gotik umgebaute Wahrzeichen Manhattans gilt als größte neogotische Kirche der Welt. Calatrava schlug vor, zusätzliche organische Strukturen aufzunehmen und eine Art »Bioshelter« in 55 Metern Höhe über dem Kirchenboden einzuziehen. Calatrava nahm Bezug auf die Verwandtschaft gotischer Säulen und Gewölbe mit Bäumen und konzipierte einen »Garten im Himmel«, der auch Reminiszenzen an den Garten Eden enthält.

Dieses ebenfalls durch zahlreiche Zeichnungen und Modelle reich dokumentierte Projekt veranschaulicht Santiago Calatravas Suche nach einer tieferen Bedeutung in der zeitgenössischen Architektur. Bei der Kirche St. John the Divine – wie auch bei den meisten anderen seiner größeren Bauvorhaben – strebt er nicht nur funktionale Lösungen an, sondern sucht auch nach symbolischen Bezügen. Diese sind nicht immer offensichtlich, resultieren sie doch aus Calatravas eigener Phantasie oder seinen skulpturalen Formen. Dennoch zeugen sie von einem Ethos, das erklären mag, warum Santiago Calatrava in kurzer Zeit zu einem der berühmtesten Architekten und Bauingenieure der Welt werden konnte. Calatrava bevorzugt den Begriff der ›Transgression‹. Ihm liegen sorgfältige Studien und praktische Erfahrungen zugrunde, und er bezieht sich auf seinen Wunsch, neue, überraschende Formen zu schaffen. Unter seinen Händen erhalten Brücken und Bahnhöfe ein neues Leben; sie lassen den nüchternen Funktionalismus hinter sich. Mit Entwürfen, die aus seinen Zeichnungen und Skulpturen entstehen, ist Santiago Calatrava auf einem besonderen kreativen Gebiet tätig, in dem nicht nur Kunst und Architektur, sondern auch Architektur und Ingenieurbau sich berühren. Daviouds Worte aus dem Jahre 1877 – »Die Vereinigung zwischen Architekt und Ingenieur muß untrennbar sein. Die Lösung wird erst dann wirklich, vollständig und fruchtbar sein, wenn Architekt und Ingenieur, Künstler und Wissenschaftler in einer Person vereinigt sind... « – stellen wahrscheinlich die anschaulichste Beschreibung des Talents von Santiago Calatrava dar.

Projects > Projets > Projekte

Santiago Calatrava's plan for the new Bilbao Airport facilities included the construction of a 42 meter high control tower, located some 270 meters from the terminal building. Inverting the normal typology for such structures, the tower is designed to have a progressively larger volume as it rises, culminating in a control deck with 360 degree visibility. Built of reinforced concrete with some aluminum cladding, the tower is symbolic of the airport itself, with its 29,000 square meter terminal facility laid out on four levels. Recalling an eyelid in elevation, and perhaps a steel-ribbed ray in plan, the structure can simultaneously handle the arrival and departure of eight aircraft through lateral wings that are intended for possible future expansion. Again, this project underlines the will of Bilbao to compete in architectural and cultural terms with southern Spanish cities such as Seville.

Santiago Calatravas Entwurf für den neuen Flughafen von Bilbao umfaßt auch den Bau eines 42 Meter hohen Towers, der in etwa 270 Metern Entfernung vom neuen Terminal errichtet wurde. In einer Umkehrung der herkömmlichen Formensprache für diesen Bautypus nimmt der Umfang des Turms nach oben hin beständig zu und gipfelt in einem Kontrollraum mit einem Panoramablick von 360 Grad. Der aus Stahlbeton errichtete Turm besitzt eine Aluminiumverkleidung und dient als Wahrzeichen des Flughafens, dessen viergeschossiges Terminalgebäude eine Fläche von 29 000 m² aufweist. Dieses Bauwerk, das im Aufriß an ein Augenlid und im Grundriß an einen Rochen aus Stahlrippen erinnert, kann mit seinen zwei Seitenflügeln – die eine spätere Ausweitung des Flughafenverkehrs bereits berücksichtigen – Ankunft und Abflug von acht Flugzeugen gleichzeitig bewältigen. Calatravas Flughafen unterstreicht den Willen der Stadt Bilbao, in architektonischer und kultureller Hinsicht mit südspanischen Städten wie Sevilla gleichzuziehen.

Les plans de Calatrava pour les nouvelles installations de l'aéroport de Bilbao comprenaient la construction d'une tour de contrôle de 42 m de haut, dressée à quelques 270 m du bâtiment du terminal. Inversant la typologie normale de ce genre de structures, la tour prend du volume au fur et à mesure qu'elle s'élève, culminant par une salle de contrôle panoramique à 360°. Construite en béton armé et partiellement recouverte d'aluminium, elle est symbolique de l'aéroport lui-même et de son terminal de 29 000 m² sur quatre niveaux. Rappelant en élévation une paupière, ou même, en plan, une raie aux arêtes d'acier, cette structure peut traiter simultanément l'arrivée et le départ de huit avions, grâce à des ailes latérales prévues pour une future extension. Une fois encore, ce projet souligne la volonté de Bilbao de concurrencer en termes d'architecture et de culture les villes du sud de l'Espagne, comme Séville.

Sondica Airport and Control Tower,
Bilbao, Spain, 1990–2000

The most visible aspect of this project is naturally the Alameda Bridge, which crosses the dry bed of the Turia River. Like a number of other Calatrava bridges, this one employs a 30 degree inclined parabolic arc made of painted steel, rising some 14 meters above the road surface at its apogee. The 26 meter wide deck spans 130 meters, just above and parallel to the underground station, also designed by Calatrava. The folding mouth-like structures that provide access to the 63 meter long subway platforms recall that Calatrava's 1981 doctoral thesis at the ETH in Zurich concerned the "Foldability of Spaceframes." Ticketing facilities are located at either end of the platforms. A ribbed roof with translucent glass openings at the level of the river bed provides daylight to the interior of the station, and signals the exterior plaza at night. The use of broken tiles in the finishing of wall surfaces recalls the tradition of Gaudí in an indirect manner.

Der auffälligste Teil dieses Projekts ist die Alameda-Brücke, die das ausgetrocknete Flußbett des Turia überspannt. Wie viele andere von Calatrava entworfene Brücken zeichnet sich auch diese durch einen Parabelbogen aus weiß lackiertem Stahl mit einem Neigungswinkel von 70 Grad aus, der sich bis zu einer Höhe von 14 Metern über der Fahrbahn erhebt. Die 26 Meter breite Brückentafel erstreckt sich über eine Länge von 130 Metern direkt oberhalb und parallel zur ebenfalls von Calatrava entworfenen U-Bahnstation. Klappbare Eingangstore sorgen für den Zugang zu den 63 Meter langen U-Bahnsteigen, an deren Enden sich die Fahrkartenschalter befinden. Die gerippten Bögen der Dachkonstruktion sind auf Höhe des Flußbettes mit Oberlichtern versehen, durch die Tageslicht ins Innere der U-Bahnstation fällt, während man nachts die Umrisse des darübergelegenen Platzes erkennen kann. Die Verwendung eines Fliesenmosaiks als Abschluß der Maueroberflächen erinnert in gewisser Hinsicht an die Bautradition des spanischen Architekten Gaudí.

L'aspect le plus spectaculaire de ce projet est tout naturellement le pont de l'Alameda qui traverse le lit à sec de la Turia. Comme un certain nombre d'autres ouvrages d'art de Calatrava, celui-ci fait appel à une arche parabolique inclinée à 30° en acier peint, qui s'élève à son apogée à 14 m au-dessus de la surface du tablier. De 26 m de large et 130 m de portée, la travée se trouve au-dessus de la station de métro, également une œuvre de l'architecte et parallèle à celle-ci. Des structures en forme de bouche donnent accès à des quais de 63 m de long. Les guichets de vente des billets sont situés aux deux extrémités. Au niveau du lit de la rivière, un toit nervuré à lanterneaux de verre translucide permet l'éclairage naturel de l'intérieur de cette station, tout en créant une animation nocturne lumineuse de la place. Les carrelages brisés du parement des murs rappellent de façon indirecte la tradition de Gaudí.

Alameda Bridge and Underground Station,
Valencia, Spain, 1991–95

Part of a plan initiated by the government of the region of Andalucia on the occasion of Expo '92, this bridge is a 200 meter span over the Meandro San Jeronimo, a branch of the Guadalquivir River. Its most striking feature is a 142 meter high pylon, inclined at an angle of 58 degrees, the same as that of the Pyramid of Cheops. Filled with cement, this tower is sufficiently massive to counterbalance the bridge deck, obviating the need for back stays. Santiago Calatrava's personal research on the Alamillo Bridge is related to a 1986 sculpture called "Running Torso" made of cubes of marble held in equilibrium by a wire under tension. His drawings of running figures also come to mind. He originally proposed a second bridge with a mirror image pylon for this site, but the client opted instead for the 500 meter long Puente de la Cartuja Viaduct, which was used as the northern entrance to the Expo '92 site. Frequently imitated by other engineers and architects, the inclined pylon of the Alamillo Bridge stands out as a symbol of modern Seville.

Diese Brücke wurde von der Regierung Andalusiens anläßlich der Expo '92 in Auftrag gegeben. Mit einer Spannweite von 200 Metern erstreckt sie sich über den Meandro San Jeronimo, einen Nebenfluß des Guadalquivir. Ihr auffälligstes Merkmal ist ein 142 Meter hoher, mit Zement gefüllter Pylon, dessen Neigungswinkel von 58 Grad dem der Cheopspyramide entspricht. Die Masse dieses Pfeilers dient als Gegengewicht für die Brückentafel und macht damit die Verwendung von Verstrebungen überflüssig. Santiago Calatravas Vorarbeiten zur Alamillo-Brücke stehen im Zusammenhang mit einer Skulptur aus dem Jahre 1986 mit dem Titel »Running Torso«, deren Marmorwürfel durch unter Spannung stehende Drahtseile im Gleichgewicht gehalten werden. Darüber hinaus erinnert der Brückenentwurf an seine Zeichnungen von Torsi in Bewegung. Ursprünglich plante Calatrava eine zweite Brücke mit einem spiegelbildlichen Pylon für dieses Gelände, aber der Auftraggeber entschied sich statt dessen für das 500 Meter lange Puenta de la Cartuja-Viadukt, das als nördlicher Eingangsbereich zum Gelände der Expo '92 diente. Der von zahlreichen anderen Ingenieuren und Architekten imitierte geneigte Pylon der Alamillo-Brücke ist ein herausragendes Symbol für das moderne Sevilla.

Ce pont de 250 m de portée qui franchit le Meandro San Jeronimo, bras du Guadalquivir, a été construit dans le cadre du plan d'urbanisme lancé par le gouvernement de la Région d'Andalousie à l'occasion d'Expo '92. Sa caractéristique la plus impressionnante est son pylône de 142 m de haut, incliné selon un angle de 58°, identique à celui de la pyramide de Chéops. Le poids de cette structure remplie de béton est suffisant pour contrebalancer celui du tablier, éliminant le besoin de haubans en arrière du pylône. L'approche très personnelle choisie par Santiago Calatrava rappelle une de ses sculptures, Torse courant (1986), composée de cubes de marbre maintenus en équilibre par un fil de fer en tension, ainsi que ses dessins de figures en pleine course. À l'origine, il avait proposé un second pont haubané à pylône identique, mais incliné dans le sens opposé, auquel le maître d'œuvre préféra le viaduc de 500 m de long de La Cartuja, qui servait d'entrée nord au site de l'Expo. Souvent repris par d'autres ingénieurs et architectes, le pylône incliné du pont de l'Alamillo est devenu un symbole de la modernité sévillane.

Alamillo Bridge and La Cartuja Viaduct,
Seville, Spain, 1987–92

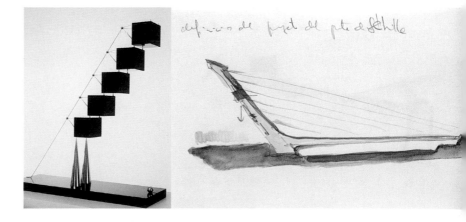

Alamillo Bridge and La Cartuja Viaduct, Seville, Spain 58 ◄ 59

The structural typology of the tree, present in projects as diverse as the Oriente Station in Lisbon, the Science Museum in Valencia and the St. John the Divine proposal, is also at the heart of the Bell Canada Enterprises Place, Gallery & Heritage Square in Toronto. Here, Calatrava worked with the New York office of corporate architects Skidmore, Owings & Merrill to create a six-story 115 meter long gallery connecting two towers with a white painted steel and glass passageway. As the New York Times said, "This gallery is nothing if not Gaudí-esque." As in the case of the New York Cathedral, with this design Calatrava reaches back to some of the roots of Western architecture, in an almost literal sense, using the image of the tree to create a great urban space with links to the Gothic tradition as well as to that of more modern figures like Gaudí.

Die Typologie des Baums, die in so unterschiedlichen Projekten wie dem Oriente-Bahnhof in Lissabon, dem Wissenschaftsmuseum in Valencia und dem Entwurf für die Kirche St. John the Divine zum Ausdruck kommt, bildet auch den Kern des Bell Canada Enterprises Place, Gallery & Heritage Square in Toronto. Bei diesem Auftrag arbeitete Calatrava mit der New Yorker Niederlassung des Architekturbüros Skidmore, Owings & Merrill zusammen. Gemeinsam errichteten sie eine sechsgeschossige, 115 Meter lange Galerie, deren zwei turmartige Hallen durch eine Passage in weiß lackiertem Stahl und Glas miteinander verbunden sind. Die New York Times schrieb dazu: »Diese Galerie wirkt wie von Gaudí geschaffen.« Wie bei der New Yorker Kirche greift Calatrava auch hier auf Grundlagen der westlichen Architektur zurück. Er gebraucht fast buchstäblich das Bild eines Baums, um einen eindrucksvollen urbanen Raum zu schaffen, der sich auf die gotische Tradition ebenso bezieht wie auf Bauten von Gaudí.

La typologie structurale de l'arbre présente dans des projets aussi divers que la gare de l'Oriente à Lisbonne, le Musée des Sciences de Valence et la proposition pour St. John the Divine, se retrouve également dans le complexe de la Bell Canada Enterprises Place, Gallery & Heritage Square à Toronto. Ici, Calatrava a travaillé en collaboration avec l'agence new-yorkaise de Skidmore, Owings & Merrill pour créer cette galerie de 115 m de long et de six étages de haut, réunissant deux tours par un passage en acier peint en blanc et en verre. Comme l'a fait remarquer le New York Times «Cette galerie tire à l'évidence son inspiration de Gaudí.» Comme pour la cathédrale de New York, Calatrava en revient ici aux racines de l'architecture occidentale, dans un sens presque littéral, se servant de l'image de l'arbre pour créer un vaste espace urbain proche de la tradition gothique comme de celle de créateurs plus récents comme Gaudi.

BCE Place, Gallery & Heritage Square,
Toronto, Canada, 1987–92

Part of a long-standing effort on the part of the government of Valencia to rehabilitate an area at the eastern periphery of the city, lodged between a large highway and the Turia River, Calatrava's City of Science took almost ten years to complete. A native of Valencia, he won a 1991 competition for the project that included a telecommunications tower perched on three elongated feet. This tower would have been the most visible element of the complex, rising to a height of 327 meters. A change in city government led to a replacement of the tower in 1996 by a music center, the Palacio de las Artes. The planetarium, with its elliptical, or rather eye-shaped plan and hemispheric dome with movable ribbed covering and an area of almost 2,600 square meters, was built between 1996 and 1998. The 241-meter-long, 41,530 square meter museum of science is based on an asymmetrical repetition of tree and rib-like forms filled with glass to admit ample daylight. With its spectacular domed Planetarium this complex is visually arresting, but for reasons independent of the architect's design, detailing of the project was not handled as skillfully as it might have been. The Palacio de las Artes and an Opera House will eventually complete the composition.

Calatravas Wissenschaftsstadt gehört zum langfristigen Sanierungsprogramm der Stadt Valencia für die östlichen Stadtrandgebiete zwischen der Autobahn und dem Flußufer der Turia; ihr Bau nahm fast zehn Jahre in Anspruch. Der aus Valencia stammende Architekt gewann den Wettbewerb von 1991 mit seinem Projekt, zu dem unter anderem ein Fernsehturm auf drei langen „Beinen" gehörte. Dieser Turm wäre mit seiner Höhe von 327 Metern das auffälligste, weithin sichtbare Element des Komplexes gewesen. Aufgrund eines Regierungswechsels im Stadtrat mußte der Turm allerdings 1996 der Konzerthalle Palacio de las Artes weichen. Das nach zweijähriger Bauzeit 1998 fertiggestellte Planetarium, dessen Kuppeldach aus beweglichen Lamellen besteht, hat einen elliptischen beziehungsweise eiförmigen Grundriß und eine Fläche von knapp 2600 m². Die äußere Gestaltung des 241 Meter langen, 41530 m² Fläche umfassenden Wissenschaftsmuseums basiert auf der asymmetrischen Wiederholung von baum- und rippenartigen Strukturen mit Glasausfachungen, durch die es mit Licht durchflutet wird. Mit seinem imposanten Planetarium bietet der Museumskomplex einen faszinierenden Anblick, obwohl die Ausführung der Details aus Gründen, die nicht auf den Entwurf zurückgehen, zu wünschen übrig läßt. Der Palacio de las Artes und ein Opernhaus werden eines Tages das architektonische Ensemble vervollständigen.

Dans le cadre d'un programme de réhabilitation conduit par la région de Valence sur une zone de la périphérie est de la ville, entre une importante autoroute et le fleuve Turia, la réalisation du projet de Cité de la Science s'est étalée sur presque dix ans. Né à Valence, Calatrava en avait remporté le concours organisé en 1991. Il comprenait alors une tour de télécommunications de 327 mètres de haut perchée sur trois pieds allongés, qui aurait été l'élément le plus spectaculaire du complexe. En 1996, un changement de municipalité a abouti au remplacement de cette tour par un centre de musique, le Palacio de las Artes. Le planétarium de plan elliptique en forme d'œil et son dôme hémisphérique à couverture mobile nervurée recouvrant une surface de près de 2600 m², a été édifié de 1996 à 1998. Le musée de la science (241 mètres de long, 41530 m²) fait appel à un principe de répétition asymétrique de formes végétales et de nervures qui constituent une immense verrière laissant passer une abondante lumière naturelle. Ce complexe est visuellement étonnant mais, pour des raisons indépendantes de l'architecte, sa réalisation n'a pas été aussi soignée qu'elle aurait dû l'être. Le Palacio de las Artes et un opéra viendront peut-être en compléter la composition.

Ciudad de las Artes y de las Ciencias, Valencia, Spain
Planetarium 1991–98
Museum 1991–2000
Palacio de las Artes 1995–

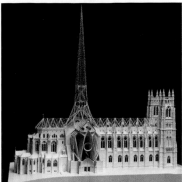

Although it remains unbuilt, this project by Santiago Calatrava is one of his most inspiring and symbolic designs. Intended as an addition to one of New York's best-known churches, originally built on neo-Romanesque lines by Heins & La Farge in 1892 and "gothicized" by Cram & Ferguson in 1911, Calatrava's project would have added a new south transept and a "bio-shelter." Obviously related in its symbolism to the original garden, the bio-shelter would be situated 55 meters above ground level, with structural elements below related to the form of the tree. Placed in the existing attic of the nave, this garden would not have changed the profile of the building, but would have brought natural light into the nave. This first prize entry in a competition was enthusiastically received both by the jury and by the public, but a lack of funding kept it from going ahead. Related, as Philip Johnson pointed out, to the original Gothic decor, the project reconciled past and future.

Obwohl nicht realisiert, zählt dieses Projekt zu Santiago Calatravas inspirierendsten und symbolträchtigsten Entwürfen. Das als Anbau an eine der berühmtesten Kirchen New Yorks geplante Bauvorhaben hätte die von Heins & La Farge 1892 im neo-romanischen Stil erbaute und 1911 von Cram & Ferguson »gotisierte« Kathedrale mit einem neuen, nach Süden gelegenen Querschiff und einem »Bioshelter« versehen. Dieser im Dachbereich des Hauptschiffs geplante Hochgarten, der symbolisch auf den Garten Eden verweist, hätte sich 55 Meter über Planum befunden, wobei die darunter befindlichen Stützen die Form eines Baums haben sollten. Die Silhouette der Kirche hätte sich dadurch nicht verändert, es wäre lediglich natürliches Licht in das Kirchenschiff gefallen. Calatravas mit dem ersten Preis ausgezeichneter Wettbewerbsbeitrag wurde sowohl von der Jury als auch in der Öffentlichkeit begeistert aufgenommen, aber finanzielle Schwierigkeiten verhinderten die Ausführung. Dieses Projekt, das, wie Philip Johnson sagt, Bezüge zum ursprünglich gotischen Erscheinungsbild aufwies, hätte die Vergangenheit mit der Zukunft in Einklang gebracht.

Même s'il n'a pas été réalisé, ce projet de Santiago Calatrava reste à ce jour l'un des plus inspirés et des plus symboliques de sa carrière. Transformation de l'une des églises new-yorkaises les plus connues, construite à l'origine en style néo-roman par Heins & La Farge en 1892 et «gothicisée» par Cram & Ferguson en 1911, ce projet aurait permis d'ajouter un nouveau transept au sud et un «bio-refuge». Évoquant symboliquement l'Eden des origines, ce refuge aurait été créé à 55 m de hauteur, au dessus d'éléments d'inspiration arborescente. Remplaçant les combles au-dessus de la nef et sans modifier le profil du bâtiment, ce jardin aurait amené davantage de la lumière naturelle à l'intérieur de la cathédrale. Ce projet, qui remporta le premier prix du concours, fut reçu avec enthousiasme à la fois par le jury et le public, mais ne put être réalisé par manque de financement. En accord avec le décor gothique d'origine – comme le fit remarquer Philip Johnson – il réconciliait le passé et le futur.

Cathedral of St. John the Divine,
New York, USA, 1991

Cathedral of St. John the Divine, New York, USA

Now under construction, this 2000-seat capacity concert hall is located at the intersection of the Tres de Mayo Avenue and Maritima Avenue in the city of Santa Cruz de Tenerife. With its distinctive concrete shell roof, in a curved triangular form culminating some 58 meters above the plaza surrounding the building, this concert hall promises to be one of the most visually spectacular structures yet designed by Calatrava. Once again, beyond the basic functions of the project, it will take on a symbolic value by the very nature of its appearance. Located on a 154 by 100 meter rectangular site, which has the particularity of including a 60 meter change in levels, the concert hall is set on a stepped platform or plinth, which contains technical facilities and changing rooms. The roof of the shell of the structure is clad in broken tile, while local volcanic stone is used for much of the paving. A 50 meter high dome covers the main hall, recalling a number of Santiago Calatrava's studies of the human eye and its lid.

Der im Bau befindliche Konzertsaal mit 2 000 Sitzplätzen liegt an der Kreuzung der Avenida Tres de Mayo und der Avenida Maritima in der Stadtmitte von Santa Cruz auf Teneriffa. Mit seinem charakteristischen dreieckigen Betonschalendach – dem Zusammenspiel von konischen und zylindrischen Formen –, das sich 58 Meter hoch über der das Gebäude umgebenden Piazza erhebt, verspricht dieser Konzertsaal, sich zu einem der spektakulärsten Bauwerke Calatravas zu entwickeln. Auch dieses Projekt erhält – abgesehen von seiner Funktion – allein schon durch sein Erscheinungsbild Symbolcharakter. Der Konzertsaal liegt auf einem 154 x 100 Meter großen, rechteckigen Gelände mit einem Niveau-Unterschied von 60 Metern. Er erhebt sich über einem terrassenartigen Sockel, der die technischen Einrichtungen und Künstlergarderoben enthält. Das Dach der Betonschale ist mit einem Fliesenmosaik verkleidet, während bei der Pflasterung der Böden Vulkangestein der Gegend Verwendung fand. Die 50 Meter hohe Kuppel über dem großen Konzertsaal erinnert an Calatravas Studien des menschlichen Auges.

Actuellement en cours de construction, cette salle de concert de 2 000 places est située au carrefour de l'avenue du Tres de mayo et de l'Avenue Maritima à Santa Cruz de Tenerife. Avec son étonnant toit en béton de forme triangulaire culminant à quelques 58 m au-dessus du niveau de la place entourant le bâtiment, cette salle devrait être l'une des structures les plus spectaculaires édifiées à ce jour par l'architecte. Allant, une fois encore, au-delà de la fonction de base du projet, il lui confère une valeur symbolique par la nature même de son aspect. Implanté sur un terrain rectangulaire de 154 x 100 m marqué par une dénivellation de 60 m, la salle est édifiée sur une plate-forme en escalier ou plinthe qui contient les installations techniques et les loges des artistes. Le «toit» est revêtu de carrelage brisé, et la plus grande partie du pavement est en pierre volcanique locale. Un dôme de 50 m de haut recouvre l'auditorium principal, rappelant un certain nombre d'études de Santiago Calatrava sur l'œil et la paupière.

Tenerife Concert Hall,
Santa Cruz de Tenerife, Canary Islands, Spain, 1991–2003

Tenerife Concert Hall, Santa Cruz de Tenerife, Canary Islands, Spain

Built for the government of Tenerife near the old city center, this project is part of a redevelopment zone for the sea front area of Santa Cruz, formerly the site of a refuse dump and an oil refinery. When Santiago Calatrava won the 1991 competition for this project, he found himself, as he often does, making a convincing case for urban renewal. A shallow arch spans a 270 meter long multi-purpose hall with a capacity of about 3000 persons, reaching a maximum height of 39 meters inside. As is most often the case in Santiago Calatrava's projects, materials change as the structure rises in space. Here, concrete darkened with local volcanic gravel gives way to steel in the design of the main arch. The flexible design of the center permits the organization of small-scale events, as well as trade shows, concerts, and the Tenerife Carnival, which is to be held there each year.

Dieser im Auftrag der Behörden von Teneriffa in der Nähe der historischen Altstadt errichtete Ausstellungssaal ist Teil eines Sanierungsvorhabens für einen Küstenstreifen von Santa Cruz, auf dem sich früher eine Mülldeponie und eine Ölraffinerie befanden. Als Santiago Calatrava 1991 die Ausschreibung für dieses Bauvorhaben gewann, plädierte er – wie so häufig – für eine Wiederbelebung des städtischen Raums. Bei diesem Projekt überspannt ein flacher Bogen eine 270 Meter lange Mehrzweckhalle für etwa 3 000 Personen, die eine Höhe von 39 Metern erreicht. Wie bei vielen von Entwürfen Calatravas findet auch hier mit steigender Höhe des Bauwerks ein Materialwechsel statt. Der im unteren Bereich verwendete Beton – durch anstehendes Vulkangestein dunkler getönt – weicht beim Hauptbogen einer Stahlkonstruktion. Das flexible Design des Ausstellungssaals ermöglicht die Organisation sowohl von kleineren Veranstaltungen als auch von Messen und Konzerten sowie des Karnevals auf Teneriffa, der hier jedes Jahr stattfinden soll.

Construit pour la municipalité de Tenerife, non loin du centre ancien de la ville, ce projet fait partie du programme de rénovation du front de mer de Santa Cruz, anciennement site d'une décharge et d'une raffinerie de pétrole. Lorsque Santiago Calatrava remporte le concours organisé pour ce projet en 1991, il propose de lui-même, comme il le fait souvent, de le transformer en une opération de rénovation urbaine. Une arche basse enjambe un hall polyvalent de 270 m de long pour une hauteur maximum de 39 m, et pouvant contenir 3 000 personnes. Comme souvent chez Calatrava, les matériaux changent au fur et à mesure que la structure s'élève dans l'espace. Dans l'arche principale, le béton, assombri par l'ajout de graviers volcaniques, cède la place à l'acier. La conception souple de ce centre permet l'organisation de petites manifestations comme de foires-expositions, de concerts et du Carnaval de Tenerife, qui s'y tient chaque année.

Tenerife Exhibition Center,
Santa Cruz de Tenerife, Canary Islands, Spain, 1992–95

It is in connection with the construction of a high-speed train line between Liège and Brussels to be completed in 2006, and its extension toward the German border, that Santiago Calatrava was chosen in a competition over Nicholas Grimshaw and Aldo Rossi to design this new facility for the Belgian city. Clearly, as Michel Daerden, Belgian Transport Minister, said in announcing the choice of Calatrava, his experience with the similar Stadelhofen Station in Zurich was essential in orienting the jury toward his project. There, as in the case of Liège, the facility is located on a hillside, and it is intended to continue the rail traffic on the line during construction. According to Santiago Calatrava, an essential feature of the new station will be its lack of a defining facade. Rather, an open plaza and an unimpeded access will highlight his own consistent principles of permeability and communication.

Nach einem Wettbewerb, aus dem er vor Nicholas Grimshaw und Aldo Rossi als Sieger hervorging, erhielt Santiago Calatrava den Auftrag zum Entwurf des neuen TGV-Bahnhofs in Lüttich. Die Anlage ist Teil einer geplanten Hochgeschwindigkeitsbahnstrecke zwischen Lüttich und Brüssel, die 2006 fertiggestellt und bis zur deutschen Grenze fortgeführt werden soll. Der belgische Verkehrsminister Michel Daerden begründete die Entscheidung für Calatrava damit, daß dessen Erfahrung mit ähnlichen Projekten wie dem Bahnhof Stadelhofen in Zürich den Ausschlag gab. Sowohl der Bahnhof in Zürich als auch der in Lüttich befinden sich in hügeligem Gelände, und in beiden Fällen sollte der Zugverkehr während der Bauarbeiten nicht unterbrochen werden. Nach Aussage des Architekten ist eines der bedeutendsten Merkmale des neuen Bahnhofs das Fehlen einer Fassade im engeren Sinne; statt dessen betonen ein Platz und der ungehinderte Zugang Calatravas Konzept der Durchlässigkeit und Kommunikation.

C'est dans le cadre de la construction d'une liaison ferroviaire à grande vitesse entre Liège et Bruxelles qui devrait être achevée en 2006 et prolongée vers l'Allemagne, que Santiago Calatrava a remporté le concours pour cette nouvelle gare, face à Nicholas Grimshaw et Aldo Rossi. Michel Daerden, ministre belge des transports, a tenu à faire savoir que l'expérience similaire de l'architecte pour la gare de Stadelhofen à Zurich avait orienté le choix du jury. Ici également, ce nouvel équipement est situé au flanc d'une colline, et le trafic ferroviaire ne doit pas être interrompu pendant la construction. Selon l'architecte, l'une des caractéristiques essentielles de cette nouvelle gare sera son absence de façade identifiable. Il s'agira plutôt d'une place ouverte et d'un accès libre qui illustreront ses principes de perméabilité et de communication auxquels il est attaché.

Liège Railway Station,
Liège, Belgium, 1996–

Intended as part of the renovation of the Lucerne railway station, this atrium structure is divided into three levels. With shopping areas on the lower level, and a restaurant above, the main atrium space serves as a mediator between the actual facade of the station and the center of the city of Lucerne where it is located. The portico itself is 109 meters long and 14 meters wide. A spectacular suspended roof, 19 meters high, sits above a set of 16 canted "anthropomorphic" F-shaped columns made of concrete and steel, which lean out over the street. The actual light steel and glass roof, supported by the columns, extends between this portico and the station facade using a triangular tensile system. The lobby created under this roof provides an airy and bright entrance, and gives ample space for pedestrian movement toward and away from the tracks.

Die im Zuge der Sanierungsarbeiten am Luzerner Bahnhof geplante Vorhalle ist in drei Nutzerebenen unterteilt. Mit einem Einkaufszentrum im unteren Geschoß und einem Restaurant im Obergeschoß dient Calatrava`s Bahnhofsvorhalle gleichsam als Vermittler zwischen dem bestehenden alten Bahnhof und der Stadt Luzern, in deren Zentrum der Bahnhof liegt. Die Vorhalle ist 109 Meter lang und 14 Meter tief. Die spektakuläre, 19 Meter hohe Dachkonstruktion aus Stahl und Glas wird mithilfe einer Dreieck-Spannvorrichtung getragen und ruht auf 16 »anthropomorphen«, Γ-förmigen Stützen aus Stahl und Beton, die über die Straße hinauskragen. Der so entstandene neue Eingangsbereich zum Bahnhof bildet einen offenen und hellen Zugang, der auch größere Passagierströme mühelos bewältigt.

Construit dans le cadre du programme de rénovation de la gare de Lucerne, cet atrium se répartit sur trois niveaux : des zones de commerces en sous-sol, un restaurant en partie haute, et un espace principal faisant lien entre la vraie façade de la gare et le centre ville de Lucerne. Le portique lui-même mesure 109 m de long pour 14 m de large. Suspendu à 19 m de hauteur, un toit spectaculaire s'appuie sur un ensemble de 16 colonnes en F «anthropomorphiques» inclinées en béton et acier, qui penche vers la rue. En verre et acier, soutenu par les colonnes, le toit léger s'étend au-delà du portique et de la façade de la gare par un système triangulaire en tension. Le hall ainsi créé constitue une entrée lumineuse, aérée et spacieuse qui facilite les mouvements des voyageurs.

Lucerne Station Hall,
Lucerne, Switzerland, 1983–89

Santiago Calatrava describes this building in anthropomorphic terms. "Its smooth shape wants to suggest an idea of welcome and hospitality," he says, "an invitation to gather and to worship. The image of two almost touching hands that dematerialize as the structure ascends." The idea of hands joined in prayer or of a forest canopy, another of Calatrava's favorite motifs, are indeed amongst the sources of more ancient cathedral designs. Here, as in so much of his other work, the architect seeks out a method that calls on the deepest sources of design, while bringing up to date the images and indeed rendering them unique. In the case of Oakland, his project is intended to "model the skyline" of the city, but also to create a deep connection to the urban environment. Indeed, he speaks of a "cathedral campus" in which the church itself become the "core element from which the different annexed buildings and exterior spaces organize themselves." Here he calls on the image of the "City of God" (Civitas Dei), an idea with very deep roots indeed in the history of spirituality.

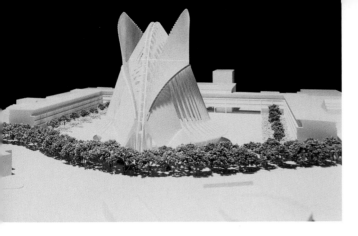

Santiago Calatrava beschreibt dieses Bauwerk mit anthropomorphischen Begriffen: »Die sanften Formen des Doms sollen eine Vorstellung von freundlicher Aufnahme und Gastlichkeit evozieren. Sie laden ein zur Versammlung und Andacht, und es ergibt sich das Bild von zwei sich fast berührenden Händen, die sich in ansteigender Gebäudelinie allmählich auflösen.« Die Idee zweier sich im Gebet vereinigender Hände oder die eines Blätterdaches, ein weiteres der von Calatrava bevorzugten Motive, entstammen dem Fundus alter Kirchenarchitektur. Der Architekt verfolgt hier, wie in so vielen anderen seiner Arbeiten, eine Methode, die sich auf die tiefsten Ursprünge des baulichen Gestaltens bezieht und die Darstellungsformen gleichzeitig auf moderne und damit unverwechselbare Weise interpretiert. Im Fall von Oakland soll sein Bauwerk die Skyline der Stadt modellieren, jedoch gleichermaßen eine enge Verbindung zum umgebenden Stadtgefüge herstellen. Tatsächlich spricht Calatrava von einer »Kathedralenanlage«, in der die Kirche selbst zum »Kernelement wird, von dem aus sich die verschiedenen umliegenden Gebäude und Außenräume organisieren«. Hierbei bezieht er sich auf die Metapher vom »Staat Gottes« (Civitas Dei), eine Idee, die sehr tief in der Geschichte der Spiritualität verwurzelt ist.

Santiago Calatrava décrit ce bâtiment en termes anthropomorphiques: «Sa forme douce veut suggérer une volonté d'accueil et d'hospitalité, une invitation à se réunir et à prier. L'image des deux mains qui se touchent presque se dématérialise au fur et à mesure que la structure s'élève.» L'idée des mains jointes en prière, ou de forêt de colonnes, autre modèle favori de Calatrava, remonte aux cathédrales médiévales. Ici, comme dans une bonne partie de son œuvre, l'architecte se penche sur les sources les plus profondes de la création, tout en se livrant à un travail d'actualisation qui donne à ses propositions un caractère unique. Le projet d'Oakland est conçu pour «intervenir sur le panorama urbain», mais également créer un lien réel avec l'environnement de la ville. Calatrava parle ici de «cathédrale-campus» : l'église elle-même est l'élément central à partir duquel s'organisent les diverses annexes et espaces extérieurs. Il s'appuie sur une imagerie liée à la «Cité de Dieu» (Civitas Dei), thème ancien tiré de l'histoire de la spiritualité.

Oakland Diocese Cathedral Campus Project,
Oakland, California, USA, 2000 (Project)

The Milwaukee Art Museum was housed in a 1957 structure designed by Eero Saarinen as a War Memorial overlooking Lake Michigan. The architect David Kahler added a large slab structure to the Museum in 1975. In 1994, the Trustees of the Milwaukee Art Museum considered a total of seventy-seven architects for a "new grand entrance, a point of orientation for visitors, and a redefinition of the museum's identity through the creation of a strong image." Santiago Calatrava won the competition with his proposal for a 27-meter-high glass and steel reception hall shaded by a moveable sunscreen (now baptized the "Burke Brise Soleil"). Included in the new spaces are 7,500 square meters of new space, of which some 1,500 square meters are set aside for temporary exhibitions. Although Calatrava generally denies specific biomorphic inspiration in his work, the Quadracci Pavilion has a decidedly bird-like quality to it, especially when the "wings" of the Brise Soleil are open. Calatrava is also responsible for the Reiman Bridge, a suspended pedestrian link between downtown and the lakefront. The noted landscape architect Dan Kiley designed public gardens for the complex.

Das Kunstmuseum Milwaukee war in einem Gebäude untergebracht, das Eero Saarinen 1957 am Ufer des Michigan-Sees errichtet hatte. Der Architekt David Kahler erweiterte es 1975 mit einem großen riegelförmigen Anbau. Im Jahr 1994 prüfte das Museumskuratorium die Entwürfe von insgesamt 77 Architekten, eingereicht in einem Wettbewerb mit der Maßgabe, einen neuen repräsentativen Eingangsbereich zu entwerfen, als „Orientierungspunkt für Besucher und Mittel zur Definition der neuen Museumsidentität durch Schaffung eines ausdrucksstarken Erscheinungsbilds". Santiago Calatrava gewann diesen Wettbewerb mit seinem Entwurf einer 27 Meter hohen Empfangshalle aus Glas und Stahl, ausgestattet mit einer beweglichen Sonnenschutzblende, die den Namen „Burke Brise-Soleil" erhalten hat. Die neuen Räumlichkeiten umfassen 7500 m² Neubauflächen, von denen 1500 m² Sonderausstellungen vorbehalten sind. Für gewöhnlich bestreitet Calatrava zwar, dass er sich von bestimmten biomorphologischen Formen inspirieren läßt, der Quadracci-Pavillon hat jedoch zweifellos Ähnlichkeit mit einem Vogel, besonders wenn die „Flügel" der Sonnenblende geöffnet sind. Calatrava hat auch die Reiman Bridge entworfen, eine Hängebrücke für Fußgänger zwischen Innenstadt und Seeufer. Den öffentlichen Park um den Museumskomplex gestaltete der bekannte Landschaftsarchitekt Dan Kiley.

Le Milwaukee Art Museum était installé depuis 1957 au bord du lac Michigan dans un bâtiment conçu à l'origine par Eero Saarinen pour un Mémorial de guerre. L'architecte David Kahler y avait ajouté une construction en dalle en 1975. En 1994, ses administrateurs ont organisé un concours auquel ont participé 77 architectes sur le thème d'une « nouvelle entrée principale, qui serve de point d'orientation pour les visiteurs et contribue à redéfinir l'identité du musée par la création d'une image forte ». Santiago Calatrava a remporté la compétition grâce à une proposition de hall de réception en verre et acier de 27 m de haut, protégé par un brise-soleil mobile, aujourd'hui baptisé « Brise-Soleil Burke ». Ce volume contient 7500 m² d'espaces nouveaux dont 1500 réservés aux expositions temporaires. Bien que Calatrava réfute généralement toute source d'inspiration biomorphique, le Quadracci Pavillon fait indéniablement penser à un oiseau, en particulier lorsque les « ailes » du brise-soleil sont déployées. L'architecte est également l'auteur du Reiman Bridge, passerelle piétonnière suspendue entre le centre et la rive du lac. Les jardins publics qui entourent ce complexe ont été dessinés par le célèbre architecte paysager David Kiley.

Extension for the Milwaukee Art Museum, Milwaukee, Wisconsin, USA, 1994–2001

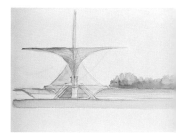

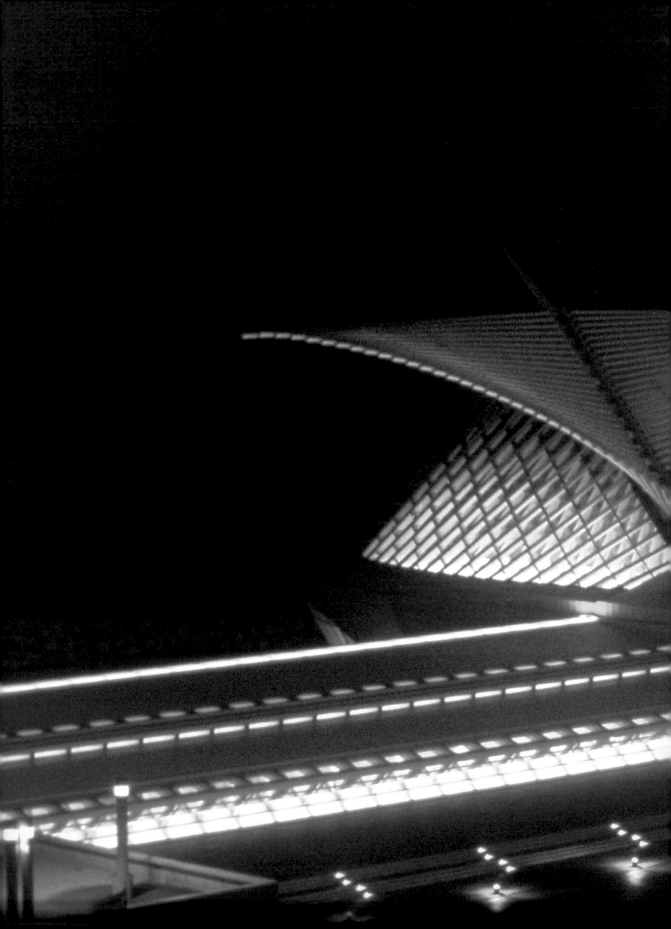

Located near the Palau Sant Jordi designed by the Japanese architect Arata Isozaki, the Montjuic Communications Tower is 130 meters high. Built like its neighbor for the 1992 Olympic Games, it is based on an inclined trunk with a semicircular element above. Although it may recall a javelin, the tower is based on Calatrava's own drawings of a kneeling figure making an offering. The base, closed by a door formed by metal blades, is related to his studies of the human eye. Acting like a sundial, the trunk projects a shadow onto the circular platform. The platform at the base is covered in broken tiles, evoking the Parque Guell by Antoni Gaudí. Related at once to the geographic and solar locations of the site, the Montjuic Tower is a symbol both of the Olympic Games and also of the progressive, artistically oriented history of Barcelona itself.

Der neben dem (von Arata Isozaki entworfenen) Palau Sant Jordi gelegene Montjuïc-Fernsehturm besitzt eine Höhe von 136 Metern. Der Turm wurde wie das Nachbarbauwerk für die Olympiade 1992 entworfen und besteht aus einem geneigten Schaft mit einem darüber befindlichen halbrunden Baukörper. Er erinnert zwar an einen Speer, basiert jedoch auf einer Zeichnung Calatravas, die eine kniende, ein Opfer darbringende Figur darstellt. Auch der über ein Tor mit Metallamellen erreichbare Sockel steht in engem Zusammenhang mit Calatravas Studien des menschlichen Auges. Wie eine Sonnenuhr wirft der Schaft einen Schatten auf die runde Plattform, die mit einem Fliesenmosaik versehen ist und Assoziationen mit dem Parco Güell von Antoni Gaudí weckt. Aufgrund seiner geographischen Lage ist der Montjuïc-Turm nicht nur ein Symbol für die Olympischen Spiele, sondern auch für die progressive künstlerische Geschichte der Stadt Barcelona.

Élevée près du Palau Sant Jordi de l'architecte japonais Arata Isozaki, la Tour de communications de Montjuïc mesure 130 m de haut. Construite comme son voisin à l'occasion des Jeux Olympiques de 1992, elle est constituée d'un tronc incliné au sommet duquel vient se fixer un important élément presque circulaire. Si elle peut évoquer un javelot, elle s'inspire en fait plutôt d'un dessin de Calatrava qui représente une figure humaine en position d'offrande. La base, fermée par une porte en lames de métal, rappelle ses études sur l'œil humain. Tel l'aiguille d'un cadran solaire, le tronc projette une ombre sur la plate-forme inférieure circulaire. Celle-ci est recouverte de carrelages brisés, rappelant les bancs du Parc Güell d'Antoni Gaudí. Étroitement liée à la géographie et à l'orientation du site, la tour de Montjuïc est à la fois le symbole des Jeux Olympiques et de l'histoire de la ville de Barcelone, marquée par l'art et l'esprit de progrès.

Montjuic Communications Tower,
Barcelona, Spain, 1989–92

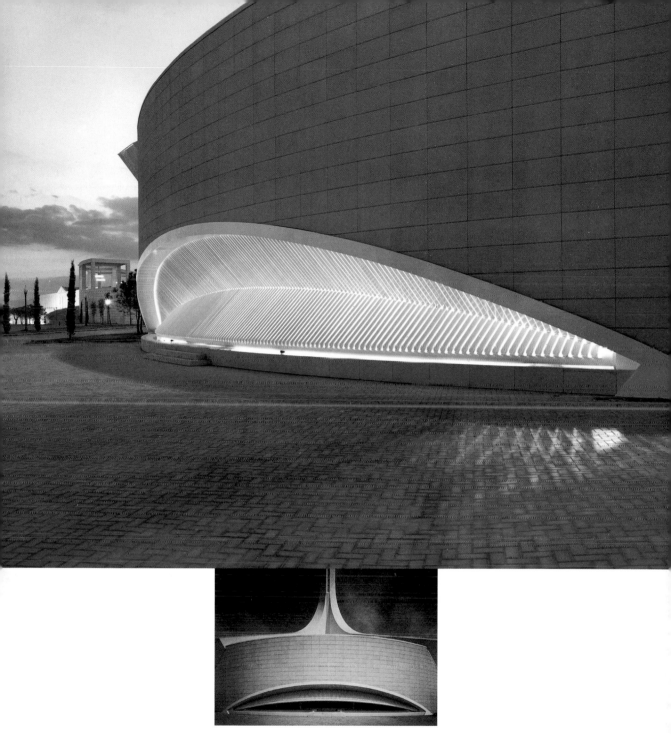

> Montjuic Communications Tower – "Génesis de la forme"

Estas gráfica del cuerpo

Génesis de la forma

experién de los pie.
eventualmente guilturos de giacometti

Part of an ambitious plan concerning the Universal Exposition of 1998 to be held in the Portuguese capital, the new train station is located about 5 kilometers from the historic center, not far from the Tago River. The most spectacular aspect of the project is undoubtedly the 78 by 238 meter covering over the eight raised railway tracks, whose typology might recall that of a forest. Rather than emphasizing the break between the city and the river implied by the station, Calatrava has sought here as elsewhere to open passageways and reestablish links. The complex includes two large glass and steel awnings over the openings, measuring no less than 112 meters in length and 11 meters in width. There are a bus station and car park, a metro station below, and a longitudinal gallery including commercial spaces included in Calatrava's brief. Ticketing and service facilities are located 5 meters below the tracks, with an atrium marking the longitudinal gallery 5 meters lower, and the opening on the river side intended as the main access point.

Der neue Bahnhof von Lissabon ist Teil eines ehrgeizigen Bauvorhabens, das im Zusammenhang mit der Weltausstellung 1998 in der portugiesischen Hauptstadt steht; er befindet sich in etwa fünf Kilometer Entfernung zur historischen Altstadt, in der Nähe des Flusses Tejo. Der spektakulärste Teil dieses Projekts ist zweifellos die 78 mal 238 Meter große Dachkonstruktion, die die acht erhöhten Gleise überspannt und an einen Wald erinnert. Wie bei all seinen Werken versuchte Calatrava auch hier, neue Wege und Durchgänge zu öffnen und Verbindungen zwischen der Stadt und dem Fluß zu schaffen, statt den Bahnhof als Hindernis zwischen diesen beiden Teilen Lissabons zu konzipieren. Der gesamte Komplex umfaßt in Calatravas Entwurf zwei große Glas– und Stahlschutzdächer über den Eingangsbereichen, die 112 Meter lang und elf Meter breit sind, sowie einen Busbahnhof, einen Parkplatz, eine U-Bahnstation und eine längs verlaufende Passage mit Gewerbeflächen. Die Fahrkartenschalter und andere Serviceeinrichtungen befinden sich fünf Meter unter den Gleisen, wobei ein Atrium die fünf Meter darunter liegende Passage prägt und die zur Flußseite gelegene Öffnung als Haupteingangsbereich dient.

Construite dans le cadre d'un ambitieux plan d'urbanisme lancé à l'occasion de l'Exposition Universelle qui se tiendra en 1998 dans la capitale portugaise, cette nouvelle gare se situe à cinq kilomètres environ du centre ville, non loin du Tage. L'aspect le plus spectaculaire de ce projet est la couverture de 78 x 238 m de surface des huit voies surélevées, dont les piliers évoquent une forêt. Plutôt que d'affirmer la rupture entre la ville et le fleuve qu'implique la station, Calatrava a cherché ici, comme ailleurs, à ouvrir des passages et rétablir des liens.
Le complexe comprend, au-dessus des ouvertures, deux grands auvents en verre et acier ne mesurant pas moins de 112 x 11 m. On trouve également une gare routière, un parking, une station de métro souterraine et une galerie commerciale en longueur, le tout prévu dans le cahier des charges. Les installations d'accueil et de vente de billets sont situées cinq mètres en dessous des voies, un atrium annonçant la galerie commerciale cinq mètres plus bas, et l'ouverture du côté de la rivière jouant le rôle d'accès principal.

Oriente Station,
Lisbon, Portugal, 1993–98

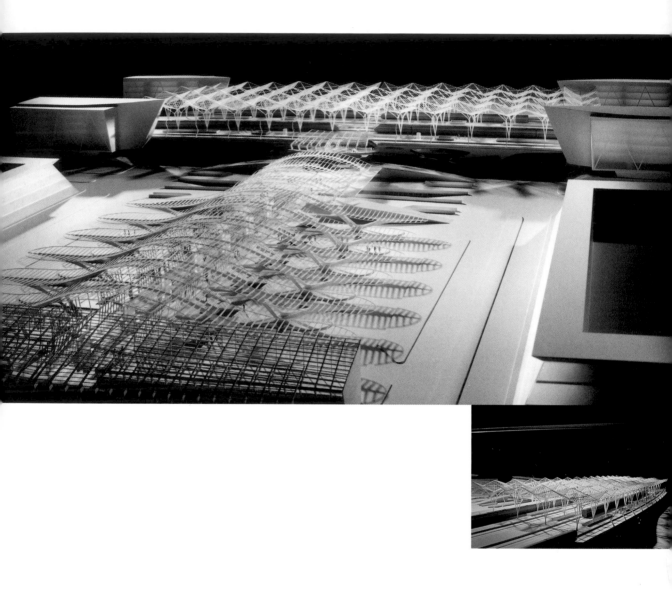

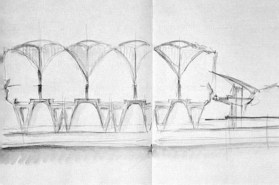

Ondarroa is a small seaport situated at the mouth of the Artibay River on the Basque coast of Spain, not far from Bilbao.
Santiago Calatrava's bridge with its single inclined arch stands like a gateway to the city, its crisp aerial outlines contrasting with the
tightly packed modern buildings that line the curved waterway. It has a 71.5 meter span with a width varying between 20.9 and
23.7 meters. The steel arch structure has an unusual pedestrian walkway, which is curved, unlike the 11 meter wide main deck,
leaving a large gap at the center between the motorway and the footpath. Walkers who prefer a more direct route can also
use the sidewalk that runs next to the road. Radiating steel braces placed every 2.86 meters carry the arch and the projecting
curved walkway, with powerful double cables reaching down vertically to hold the road deck. This bridge, together with
those in Valencia and Orleans, is of a typology recently developed by Calatrava.

Ondarroa ist eine kleine Hafenstadt an der Mündung des Artibay und liegt in der Nähe von Bilbao an der baskischen Küste Spaniens. Santiago Calatravas Brücke mit ihrem einzelnen, geneigten Bogen erinnert an ein Stadttor und hebt sich mit ihren klar umrissenen Konturen deutlich von der dichten modernen Bebauung ab, die sich entlang des kurvenreichen Flußlaufes erstreckt. Die Brücke hat eine Spannweite von 71,5 Metern und eine Breite zwischen 20,9 und 23,7 Metern. Die Stahlbogenkonstruktion verfügt über einen ungewöhnlichen Fußgängerweg, dessen Linienführung der elf Meter breiten Brückentafel nicht durchgehend folgt, wodurch in der Mitte eine große Lücke zwischen Fahrbahn und Fußgängerweg entsteht. Passanten, die die Brücke rasch überqueren möchten, können auch den neben der Fahrbahn gelegenen Gehweg benutzen. Die in Abständen von 2,86 Metern plazierten fächerförmigen Stahlverstrebungen stützen den Bogen und den herausragenden geschwungenen Fußgängerweg, wobei mächtige vertikale Doppelstahlseile die Fahrbahn tragen. Diese Brücke gehört, ebenso wie die Entwürfe von Valencia und Orleans, einem erst kürzlich von Calatrava entwickelten Brückentypus an. Zu seinen Kennzeichen zählt die horizontale Tragekonstruktion, die als Queraussteifung des Konstruktionssystems dient und sie damit gegen Torsionsspannungen beständig macht sowie das Risiko einer Torsionsverzerrung minimiert. Das System ermöglicht die in Relation zur Brückentafel asymmetrische Plazierung des Bogens.

Ondarroa est un petit port de mer situé à l'embouchure de l'Artibay sur la côte basque, non loin de Bilbao. Ce pont à arche unique inclinée joue le rôle de porte d'entrée vers la ville, son profil aérien et nerveux contrastant avec l'alignement des immeubles modernes le long de la courbe du fleuve. Il offre une portée de 71,5 m pour une largeur variant de 20,9 à 23,7 m. Le profil de l'arche en acier semble repousser de côté une curieuse passerelle piétonnière en courbe, alors que le tablier principal de 11 m de large est rectiligne, un large vide étant ménagé en partie centrale entre la circulation des voitures et celle des piétons. Les promeneurs qui préfèrent un cheminement plus direct peuvent également utiliser le trottoir qui longe la route. Des haubans d'acier radiants accrochés tous les 2,86 m soutiennent l'arche et la passerelle courbe, tandis que le tablier de la route est accroché à de solides câbles doubles verticaux. Ce pont, comme ceux de Valence et d'Orléans, relève d'une typologie récemment mise au point par Calatrava, dans laquelle la structure porteuse horizontale du pont agit comme un raidisseur du système structural, lui permettant de résister aux contraintes de torsion et minimisant la déformation par torsion. Ce système permet à l'arche d'occuper une position asymétrique par rapport au tablier.

Nuevo acceso al puerto de Ondarroa,
Ondarroa, Spain, 1989–95

It was decided to build the Reichstag at the eastern end of the Königsplatz in Berlin in 1871, but it was Paul Wallot, and not the original competition winner, Friedrich Bohnstedt, who began the actual work ten years later. In June 1992, another competition, almost as controversial as the first, was launched to refurbish the highly symbolic fire- and war-damaged structure. The three preliminary winners – the Dutch architect Pi de Bruijn, who was an unexpected first prize choice, Sir Norman Foster and Santiago Calatrava – were asked at the end of April 1993 to amend their original proposals, but it was Calatrava who came closest in the first round to finding the definitive solution. His extremely light dome with an 18 meter aperture above the assembly hall was apparently very similar to the scheme finally adopted by the competition winner Foster. In Calatrava's design the original structure of the Reichstag was to be carefully laid bare, and its inside spaces were conceived to be as pure and light flooded as possible.

To avoid filling the interior too much, he proposed to create a new office block behind the Reichstag for the parties' representatives. This area, which he named the Dorotheenblock, is now to be built by Pi de Bruijn.

Im Jahre 1871 fiel der Beschluß, den Reichstag am östlichen Ende des Königsplatzes in Berlin zu errichten; aber nicht der ursprüngliche Gewinner des Architekturwettbewerbs, Friedrich Bohnstedt, sondern Paul Wallot begann zehn Jahre später mit den Bauarbeiten. Im Juni 1992 fand eine neue, fast ebenso heftig umstrittene Ausschreibung zur Sanierung des symbolträchtigen, von Feuer und Krieg gezeichneten Gebäudes statt. Die drei Gewinner der Vorrunde – der niederländische Architekt Pi de Bruijn (eine überraschende Wahl), Sir Norman Foster und Santiago Calatrava – wurden Ende April 1993 um eine Überarbeitung ihrer ursprünglichen Entwürfe gebeten. Calatrava war bereits in der ersten Runde der endgültigen Lösung am nächsten gekommen. Sein Entwurf einer extrem leichten Kuppel mit einer Öffnung von 18 Metern über dem Sitzungssaal wies einige Ähnlichkeit mit den von Foster – dem Wettbewerbsgewinner – später entwickelten Plänen auf. Calatravas Kuppel sollte sich öffnen können – ein ungewöhnliches Detail einer Konstruktion, deren Hauptmerkmal Spannung und nicht Druck ist. Sein Entwurf sah vor, die ursprüngliche Bausubstanz des Reichstags vorsichtig freizulegen; die Innenräume waren so konzipiert, daß sie möglichst klar und lichtdurchflutet wirkten. Um den Innenraum nicht zu sehr auszufüllen, schlug Calatrava den Bau eines hinter dem Reichstag gelegenen Bürokomplexes für die Räumlichkeiten der verschiedenen Parteien vor. Dieser Bereich, der Dorotheenblock, wird nun von Pi de Bruijn gebaut.

C'est en 1871 que fut prise la décision de construire le Reichstag à l'extrémité est de la Königsplatz, mais ce fut Paul Wallot, et non le gagnant initial du concours, Friedrich Bohnstedt, qui entama les travaux de construction, dix ans plus tard. En juin 1992, un autre concours, aux résultats presque aussi controversés que le premier, fut lancé pour restaurer le bâtiment gravement endommagé par l'incendie historique et la guerre. Les trois premiers architectes sélectionnés, le Néerlandais Pi de Bruijn, premier prix inattendu, Norman Foster et Santiago Calatrava se virent demander à la fin du mois d'avril 1993 de modifier leurs propositions, mais Calatrava s'était le plus approché de la solution finalement retenue. Son dôme aérien de 18 m d'ouverture au-dessus de la salle des sessions était apparemment très semblable au projet finalement proposée par le vainqueur final du concours, Foster. Le dôme de Calatrava devait s'ouvrir et se fermer, configuration rare pour une structure qui agit en tension et non en compression. Dans ce projet, la structure originale du Reichstag était soigneusement vidée et les espaces intérieurs devaient être aussi épurés et lumineux que possible. Pour éviter de trop surcharger l'intérieur, il avait proposé de créer un nouveau bâtiment de bureaux pour les députés, à l'arrière du bâtiment ancien. Ce projet qu'il avait nommé Dorotheenblock sera conçu par Pi de Bruijn.

Reichstag Conversion,
Berlin, Germany, 1992

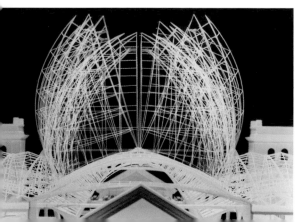

With its overall length of 128 meters and its twin inclined and split arches, this bridge was one of the first to contribute to the reputation of Santiago Calatrava. Crossing a kind of no-man's land originally created by the existence of railway lines, the bridge links the Bach de Roda and Felipe II streets, reconnecting a large section of the city to the sea. Its recognizable form is a testimony to the accuracy of the theory of Calatrava that peripheral urban areas can indeed be generated by such a symbolic intervention. Combining powerful concrete supports and a steel arch structure that grows progressively lighter as it rises, the Bach de Roda–Felipe II bridge also demonstrates Calatrava's adherence to a hierarchy of materials and forms, chosen in relation to their distance from the ground. Despite its very different structural nature the Lyon-Satolas Airport Railway Station employs a similar hierarchy.

Diese Brücke mit einer Gesamtlänge von 129 Metern und zwei schrägstehenden und geteilten Bögen trug als eines der ersten Bauwerke zu Santiago Calatravas Ruhm bei. Calatravas Konstruktion überquert ein Stück Niemandsland zwischen Bahngleisen, verbindet die Straßen *Bach de Roda* und *Felipe II* miteinander und gibt damit einem großen Stadtgebiet wieder Zugang zum Meer. Der hohe Wiedererkennungswert der Brückenform ist ein Beweis für die Richtigkeit von Calatravas These, daß Stadtrandgebiete sich durch einen solchen symbolischen Eingriff aufwerten lassen. Durch die Kombination von mächtigen Betonpfeilern und einer Stahlbogenkonstruktion, die mit zunehmender Höhe immer leichter zu werden scheint, dokumentiert die Bach de Roda–Brücke gleichzeitig Calatravas Verbundenheit mit einer Hierarchie von Materialien und Formen, die je nach Abstand zum Boden Einsatz finden. Ungeachtet seiner gänzlich anderen Konstruktionsweise ist auch der TGV Bahnhof Lyon-Satolas von einer ähnlichen Hierarchie geprägt.

Avec sa longueur totale de 128 m et ses arches jumelles inclinées ouvertes, ce pont a été l'un des premiers à contribuer à la réputation de Santiago Calatrava. Franchissant une sorte de no-man's land ferroviaire, il relie les rues Bach de Roda et Felipe II, rapprochant une vaste partie de la ville à la mer. Sa forme reconnaissable témoigne de la valeur de la théorie de Calatrava selon laquelle des zones périphériques urbaines peuvent revenir à la vie par des interventions symboliques de ce type. Associant de puissants piliers de béton et une structure en arche métallique qui s'amincit au fur et à mesure qu'elle s'élève, l'ouvrage démontre également le penchant de l'architecte pour une hiérarchie des formes et des matériaux, en fonction de leur éloignement du sol. Même si la nature de sa structure est très différente, la gare de Lyon-Satolas fait appel à une hiérarchie similaire.

Bach De Roda–Felipe II Bridge,
Barcelona, Spain, 1984–87

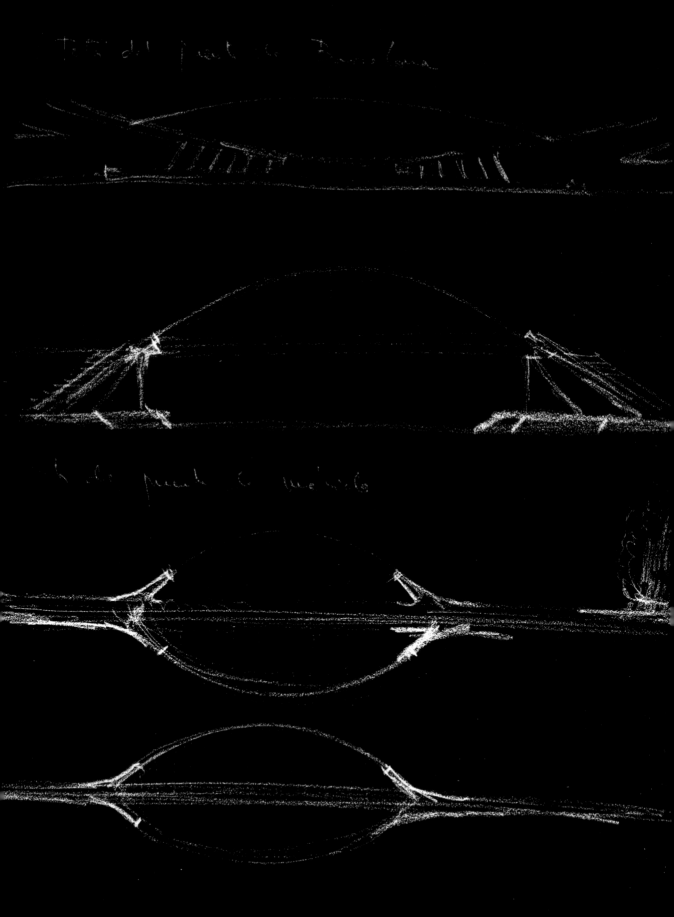

It was as a result of winning the competition for this station that Santiago Calatrava established his offices in Zurich. Located against a curved, green embankment near the Bellevue-Platz and not far from the Theater-Strasse, the Stadelhofen Railway Station is close to the city center, and to the Zurich-See. The station stretches some 270 meters (with a width of 40 meters), revealing its structure only as the traveler reaches the train tracks themselves. Approached through a series of pedestrian streets, the first visible sign of the station is a nineteenth century building, preserved because of its value in terms of the local context. Below ground, a parallel shopping area, whose ribbed concrete design may appear to be anthropomorphic, follows the curve of the tracks themselves. Mouth-like hatches or doorways lead downward toward this commercial zone. Santiago Calatrava's drawings typically reveal no dinosaur-like shapes for this station, but rather such practical inspiration as the form of the human hand that he adopted for the inclined columns.

Die Tatsache, daß Calatrava die Ausschreibung für den Bahnhof Stadelhofen gewann, bewog ihn u.a. zur Gründung seines Architekturbüros in Zürich. Dieser Bahnhof liegt mitten in der Stadt und grenzt an ein geschwungenes, abschüssiges Gelände in der Nähe des Bellevue-Platzes und der Theaterstraße. Das Bahnhofsgebäude erstreckt sich über eine Länge von 270 Metern (und eine Breite von 40 Metern) und offenbart seine Konstruktionsweise erst in dem Moment, in dem der Reisende den Bahnsteigbereich betritt. Das erste sichtbare Zeichen des über mehrere Fußgängerzonen erreichbaren Bahnhofs ist ein Gebäude aus dem 19. Jahrhundert, das erhalten blieb und restauriert wurde. Im Untergeschoß befindet sich ein Einkaufszentrum, das parallel zu den Gleisen im darüberliegenden Geschoß verläuft und dessen Stahlbetondecke anthropomorphe Formen aufweist. Der Zugang zu diesem Einkaufsbereich erfolgt über klappbare Luken und nach unten führende Treppen. Calatravas ursprünglicher Entwurf für diesen Bahnhof zeigt keine »dinosaurierartigen« Formen; statt dessen ließ sich der Architekt bei der Gestaltung der geneigten Säulen von der Form der menschlichen Hand inspirieren.

C'est parce qu'il avait remporté le concours de cette gare que Santiago Calatrava installa son agence à Zurich. Située au flanc d'une colline boisée près de Bellevue-Platz et non loin de la Theater Strasse, la gare du Stadelhofen est proche du centre et du lac de Zurich. Elle s'étend sur 270 m environ (pour une largeur de 40 m), et ne révèle sa structure au voyageur que lorsqu'il atteint les quais. On y accède par une série de volées piétonnières, et le premier signe visible de sa présence est un bâtiment du XIXe siècle, préservé pour sa signification dans le contexte local. En sous-sol, un centre commercial, dont les voûtes nervurées peuvent sembler anthropomorphique, se développe en parallèle à la courbe des voies. Des accès en forme de bouches permettent de descendre vers ces espaces commerciaux. Les esquisses préparatoires de Calatrava ne jouent pas avec les formes d'un quelconque animal préhistorique, mais tirent plutôt leur inspiration de la forme de la main, qu'il a adoptée pour ses colonnes inclinées.

Stadelhofen Railway Station,
Zurich, Switzerland, 1983–90

le sujet de les mains
parcours de la force... deteuxement
et geste –

Stadelhofen Railway Station, Zurich, Switzerland   142 ◄ 143

Despite its obvious similarity to a sort of prehistoric bird, the shape of this 5,600 square meter facility, which was designed for the French national railway company (SNCF) serving to connect the high-speed train network (TGV) to the Lyon Airport at Satolas, is more closely related to Calatrava's sculptures than to any animal. The winged design recalls Eero Saarinen's TWA Terminal at Kennedy Airport (1957–62), but its function and aspects such as the 500 meter long covered platform for the trains differentiate it from its predecessor in a decisive manner. Built at a total cost of 600 million francs in three phases, the station accommodates six tracks, with the middle two encased in a concrete shell for trains that pass through at high speed without stopping. A 180 meter long connecting bridge linking the facility to the airport terminal itself gives the plan a shape that might bring to mind a stingray as much as a bird. Its essential feature remains the main hall, with its 1,300 ton roof, measuring 120 meters by 100, with a maximum height of 40 meters.

Trotz seiner Ähnlichkeit mit einem prähistorischen Vogel steht die Form des 5600 m² großen Bahnhofs – der für die Französische Staatsbahn SNCF konzipiert wurde und das wachsende Netz von Hochgeschwindigkeitszügen (TGV) mit dem Flughafen Lyon-Satolas verbinden soll – in einem engeren Bezug zu Calatravas Skulpturen. Calatravas Entwurf in Form eines zum Flug ansetzenden Vogels erinnert an Eero Saarinens TWA-Terminal am John F. Kennedy Airport (1956–62), aber seine Funktion sowie verschiedene Bauteile wie etwa der 500 Meter lange, überdachte Bahnsteig unterscheiden das Bauwerk deutlich von seinem Vorgänger. Der Bahnhof wurde in drei Phasen mit einem Budget von 600 Millionen Francs errichtet. Er beherbergt sechs Gleise, wobei die beiden mittleren für Hochgeschwindigkeitszüge mit Spitzengeschwindigkeiten von über 300 Kilometern pro Stunde von einer Betonhülle umgeben sind. Die 180 Meter lange Brücke, die den Bahnhof mit dem Flugenhafenterminal verbindet, gibt dem Bauwerk eine Form, die gleichermaßen an einen Rochen wie an einen Vogel erinnert. Das herausragendste Merkmal des Bahnhofs ist jedoch die 120 Meter lange, 100 Meter breite und 40 Meter hohe Eingangshalle mit ihrer 1300 Tonnen schweren Dachkonstruktion.

Même si elle fait penser à une sorte d'oiseau préhistorique, la forme de ce bâtiment de 5 600 m², conçu pour la SNCF pour connecter le réseau des trains à grande vitesse à l'aéroport de Lyon-Satolas, rappelle davantage les sculptures de l'architecte qu'un quelconque animal. Le dessin en aile évoque également le terminal TWA réalisé par Eero Saarinen à Kennedy Airport (1957–62), mais sa fonction et divers aspects, comme ses quais couverts de 500 m de long, le différencient radicalement de ce prédécesseur. Construite en trois phases pour un coût total de 600 millions de F, la gare couvre six voies, dont les deux centrales réservées aux trains passant à grande vitesse sont isolées par une coquille de béton. Une passerelle de 180 m de long relie ces installations au terminal de l'aéroport et donne à leur plan une forme qui évoque une raie manta ou un oiseau. La particularité essentielle reste le hall principal recouvert d'un toit de 1300 tonnes, mesurant 120 m de long par 100 de large pour une hauteur maximum de 40 m.

Lyon-Saint Exupéry Airport Railway
Station, Lyon, France, 1989–94

Lyon-Saint Exupéry Airport Railway Station, Lyon, France   148 ◂ 149

ojo avido

ira certero, preciso, incisivo

instrumento físico organo

orden de consideración de

estima del equilato

expresión fija s la muerte descaso

mudo de las ideas cuya expresión

plita e inmediata s el gesto de

el ojo sable

el exte

el ojo s a

el interio el ojo

el orden de la intuición el orden del pensamiento

consisten crean otra imagen juzga y controla

aquellos resultados y prendidos

idas

sculptor

externo

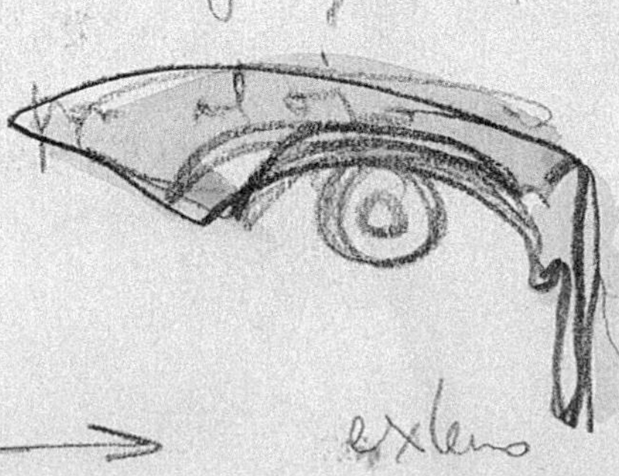

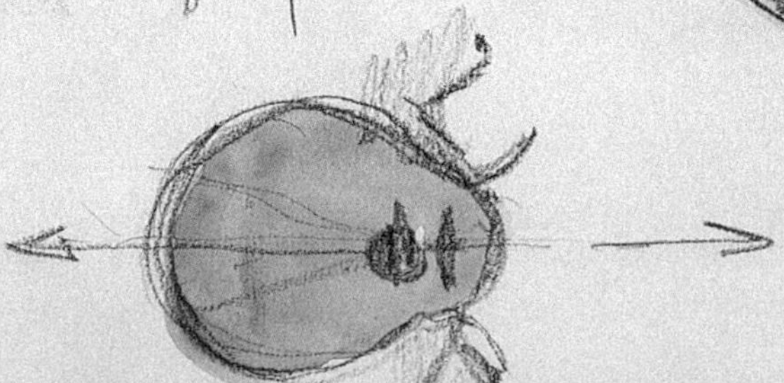

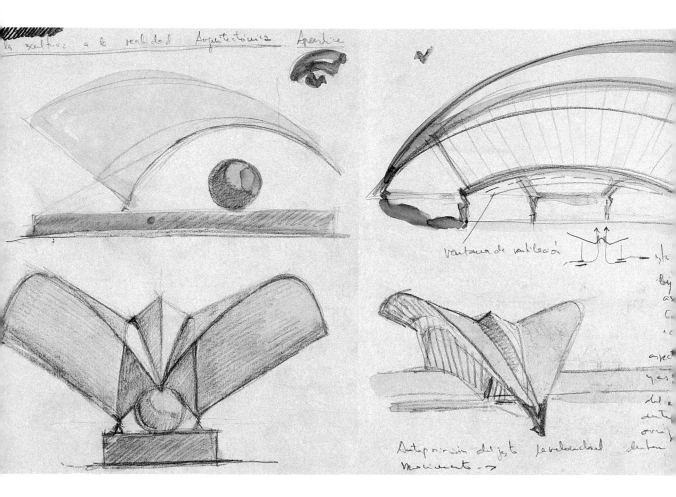

Lyon-Saint Exupéry Airport Railway Station, Lyon, France

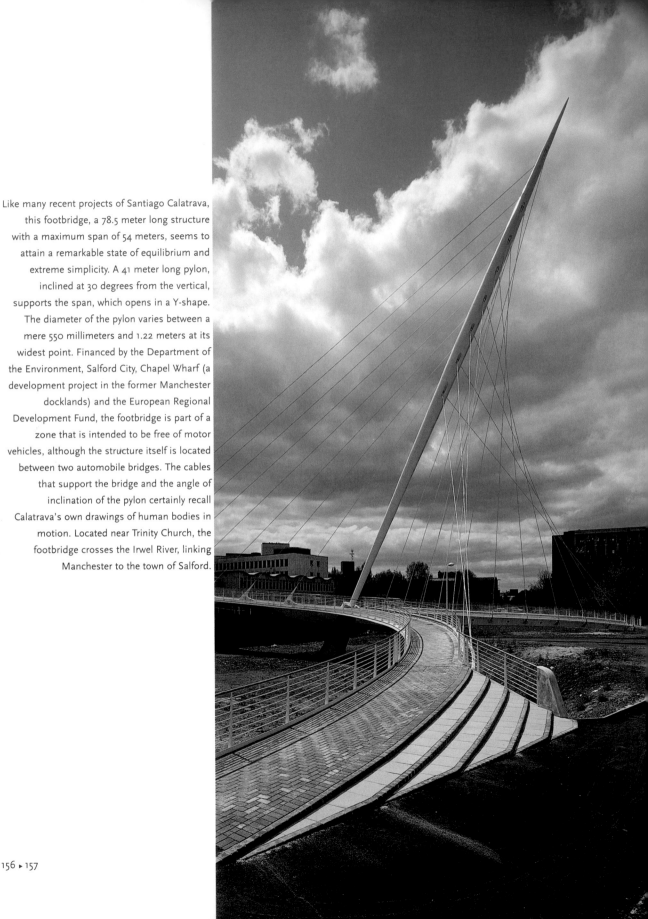

Like many recent projects of Santiago Calatrava, this footbridge, a 78.5 meter long structure with a maximum span of 54 meters, seems to attain a remarkable state of equilibrium and extreme simplicity. A 41 meter long pylon, inclined at 30 degrees from the vertical, supports the span, which opens in a Y-shape. The diameter of the pylon varies between a mere 550 millimeters and 1.22 meters at its widest point. Financed by the Department of the Environment, Salford City, Chapel Wharf (a development project in the former Manchester docklands) and the European Regional Development Fund, the footbridge is part of a zone that is intended to be free of motor vehicles, although the structure itself is located between two automobile bridges. The cables that support the bridge and the angle of inclination of the pylon certainly recall Calatrava's own drawings of human bodies in motion. Located near Trinity Church, the footbridge crosses the Irwel River, linking Manchester to the town of Salford.

Wie viele andere der von Santiago Calatrava in den letzten Jahren entworfenen Bauten zeichnet sich auch diese Fußgängerbrücke in der Nähe der Trinity Church – eine 78,5 Meter lange Konstruktion mit einer maximalen Spannweite von 54 Metern, die sich über den Fluß Irwel erstreckt und Manchester mit Salford verbindet – durch bemerkenswerte Schlichtheit und besondere Ausgewogenheit aus. Der 41 Meter hohe, um 30 Grad von der Senkrechten abweichende Pylon trägt die Y-förmige Brückentafel, wobei sein Durchmesser zwischen 550 Millimetern und 1,22 Metern an seiner breitesten Stelle variiert. Die vom Umweltdezernat der Stadt Salford, Chapel Wharf (einem Erschließungsgebiet innerhalb der ehemaligen Hafenanlagen von Manchester) und aus europäischen Förderungsmitteln finanzierte Fußgängerbrücke ist Teil einer geplanten autofreien Zone – obwohl sich die Konstruktion genau zwischen zwei für den Autoverkehr bestimmten Brücken befindet. Die Stahlseile und der Neigungswinkel des Pylons erwecken deutliche Assoziationen zu Calatravas Zeichnungen von menschlichen Körpern in Bewegung.

Comme c'est le cas dans de nombreux projets récents de S. Calatrava, cette passerelle piétonnière de 78,5 m de long pour une portée centrale de 54 m semble atteindre à un remarquable équilibre et à une simplicité extrême. Le pylône de 41 m de haut, incliné à 30° par rapport à la verticale, soutient le tablier qui s'ouvre en Y. Le diamètre du pylône varie de 550 mm à 1,22 m. Financé par le Département de l'Environnement, la ville de Salford, Chapel Wharf (un programme de rénovation urbaine dans les anciens docks de Manchester) et le Fond européen de développement régional, cette passerelle s'inscrit dans une zone interdite à la circulation automobile, même si elle se trouve intercalée entre deux ponts réservés aux voitures. Les câbles qui soutiennent le tablier et l'angle d'inclinaison du pylône rappellent certains dessins de l'architecte sur le thème du corps humain en mouvement. Située près de Trinity Church, la passerelle franchit l'Irwel, et relie Manchester à la ville de Salford.

Trinity Bridge,
Salford, England, 1993–95

Trinity Bridge, Salford, England   158 ◄ 159

This inclined parabolic arch structure has a span of 71 meters. The steel uprights that run from the arch to the deck of the bridge every 5.7 meters do give an impression of frozen movement, perhaps that of a pendulum, as Sergio Polano has suggested. Serving to link a run-down commercial area called Uribitarte with the city of Bilbao across the Bilbao River, the Campo Volantin Footbridge is one aspect of a vast campaign of urban renewal, which includes Frank Gehry's recently inaugurated Guggenheim Bilbao Museum, subway stations by Sir Norman Foster, and Calatrava's own Sondica Airport project. As in many other designs by Santiago Calatrava, an apparent disequilibrium or rather a sense of frozen movement is heightened by the lightness of the structure. The symbolic importance of the bridge, which may indeed have an influence on urban renewal, is emphasized by its spectacular night lighting.

Diese geneigte Parabelbogenkonstruktion besitzt eine Spannweite von 75 Metern. Die Stahlstützen, die die Brückentafel in Abständen von jeweils 5,7 Metern mit dem Bogen verbinden, erzeugen den Eindruck eines in der Bewegung erstarrten Gebildes – möglicherweise eines Pendels (nach Ansicht Sergio Polanos). Die den Fluß Bilbao überquerende Campo Volantin-Fußgängerbrücke dient als Verbindung zwischen dem Industriegebiet Uribitarte und der Innenstadt von Bilbao. Sie ist nur Teil eines umfangreichen Stadtsanierungsprogramms, das auch Frank Gehrys vor kurzem eröffnetes Guggenheim Bilbao Museum, mehrere U-Bahnstationen von Sir Norman Foster und Calatravas Flughafen Sondica umfaßt. Wie bei vielen seiner Entwürfe wird auch bei dieser Brücke die scheinbar heikle Balance oder der Eindruck einer erstarrten Bewegung durch die Leichtigkeit der Konstruktion verstärkt, während die symbolische Bedeutung der Brücke – die möglicherweise tatsächlichen Einfluß auf eine städtische Erneuerung ausübt – durch die spektakuläre nächtliche Beleuchtung besonders zum Ausdruck kommt.

Cet ouvrage à arche parabolique inclinée présente une portée de 71 m. Les montants verticaux en acier qui relient l'arche au tablier tous les 5,7 m donnent une impression de mouvement gelé, faisant éventuellement penser à celui d'un pendule, comme l'a suggéré Sergio Polano. Reliant un quartier commercial en décrépitude appelé Uribitarte à la ville de Bilbao, de l'autre côté du fleuve, cette passerelle fait partie d'une vaste opération de rénovation urbaine qui comprend le Guggenheim Bilbao Museum de Frank Gehry, récemment inauguré, des stations de métro signées Norman Foster, et le projet de l'aéroport de Sondica, également de Calatrava. Comme dans de nombreux autres projets de celui-ci, le déséquilibre apparent ou mieux, le sentiment de mouvement bloqué, est souligné par la légèreté de la structure. L'importance symbolique du pont, qui devrait certainement exercer une influence sur le renouveau urbain de cette zone, est mise en valeur par un spectaculaire éclairage nocturne.

Campo Volantin Footbridge,
Bilbao, Spain, 1990–97

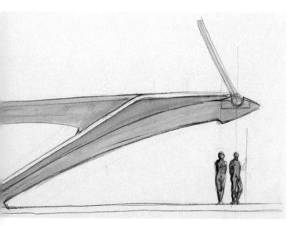

Built at a total cost of $30 million, the daring Orléans bowstring bridge has an overall length of 378 meters and a main span of 201.6 meters, supported by a single inclined arch. Both this arch and the bridge itself are made of steel. The steel in the Orléans Bridge weighs 5,380 tons or 552 kilos per meter. The cost of the steel alone was over $13 million. The client for this project was the Communauté de l'Agglomération Orléanaise (CCAO). As he often has in the past, Calatrava drew on the latest techniques for the construction of this bridge. The arch was erected using mobile cranes placed on the bridge deck before the load was transferred to the three-branch concrete supports. Calatrava won the competition for the construction of this bridge over the Loire River linking the communities of Saint-Jean de la Ruelle in the north and Saint-Pryvé Saint-Mesmin in the south in 1996. Referring in his design to the existing Pont Royal or Pont George V, Calatrava nonetheless succeeded in creating a thoroughly modern bridge for this French city.

Die Baukosten der gewagten Zugbandbogenkonstruktion der Brücke in Orléans beliefen sich auf 30 Millionen Dollar. Die Brücke ist 378 Meter lang, die größte, von einem einzigen geneigten Stahlbogen gestützte Spannweite beträgt 201,6 Meter. Die ganze Brücke besteht aus Stahl – insgesamt 5380 Tonnen oder 552 Kilogramm Stahl pro Brückenmeter. Die Kosten für den Stahl allein betrugen über 13 Millionen Dollar. Bauherr dieses Projekts war die Communauté de l'Agglomération Orléanaise (CCAO, Region Orléans). Wie schon so oft zuvor, hat Calatrava sich auch hier der neuesten Bautechniken bedient. Der Stahlbogen wurde mit Hilfe von auf dem Brückendeck installierten fahrbaren Kränen aufgerichtet, bevor seine ganze Last von den dreibeinigen Betonpfeilern aufgenommen wurde. Den Wettbewerb für diese Brücke über die Loire als Verbindung zwischen den Stadtteilen Saint-Jean de la Ruelle im Norden und Saint-Pryvé Saint-Mesmin im Süden gewann Calatrava 1996. Obwohl er sich gestalterisch auf die bestehenden Brücken – Pont Royal und Pont George V – bezog, gelang es dem Architekten, der Stadt Orléans eine vollkommen moderne Brücke zu bauen.

Commande de la Communauté de l'Agglomération Orléanaise (CCAO) et réalisé pour un budget de $30 millions, cet audacieux pont en arc tendu offre une longueur de 378 mètres et une arche principale de 201,6 mètres soutenue par un arc unique incliné. L'ensemble est en acier (5380 tonnes, soit 552 kilos par mètre). Le coût du seul matériau a dépassé $13 millions. Comme souvent dans le passé, Calatrava a fait appel aux techniques les plus récentes. L'arc a été élevé en utilisant des grues mobiles positionnées sur le tablier du pont avant que la charge ne soit transférée aux supports à trois branches en béton. Le concours pour la construction de ce pont sur la Loire, entre Saint-Jean de la Ruelle et Saint Pryvé-Saint Mesmin, avait été remporté en 1996. Bien qu'il se réfère pour la conception au Pont-Royal et au Pont George V, Calatrava est néanmoins parvenu à créer un pont tout à fait moderne pour la ville d'Orléans.

Bridge of Europe, Orléans,
France, 1996–2000

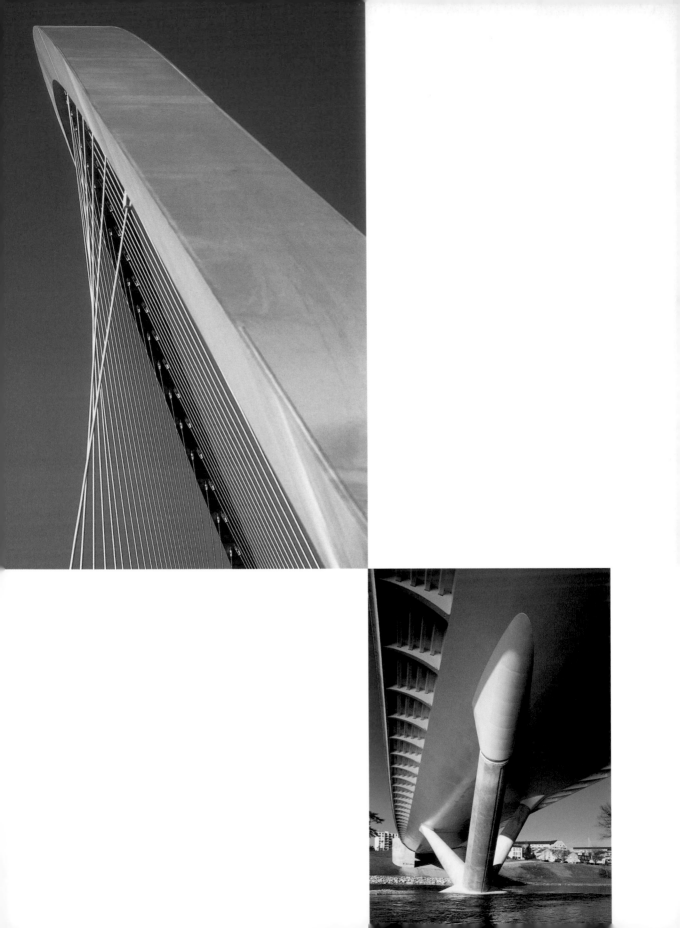

Santiago Calatrava was called on to participate actively in the work for the August 2004 Summer Olympics to be held in Marousi, a northern suburb of Athens. His intervention concerns new roofs for the Olympic Stadium and Velodrome; the creation of plazas and canopies for the entire complex; and numerous other facilities. The Olympic Stadium will be covered with a roof of laminated glass, composed of a pair of bent "leaves," which will cover a surface of 25,000 square meters. The load bearing structure of each leaf is comprised of double-tied arches made of tubular steel, which span 304 meters in length and rise to a height of 60 meters. The Velodrome will be covered with a roof that is wood-clad on the interior (for acoustical purposes) and metal-covered on the exterior, with a central area of sun-protected laminated glass. 145 meters long by 100 meters wide and rising to a height of 45 meters, the roof will shield the athletes from potentially disruptive winds. Calatrava is also working on the open spaces, featuring circulation spines, a curving enclosed Agora, a central Plaza of the Nations, and landscaped areas. Four entrance plazas will provide ceremonial access to the Athens Olympic Sports Complex, and the architect is also creating a 110-meter-tall movable steel sculpture in the form of a spindle, and a "Nations Wall" or movable tubular steel wall sculpture, 250 meters long by 20 meters high, mounted 5 meters off the ground.

Santiago Calatrava wurde zur Mitgestaltung der Anlagen für die Olympischen Sommerspiele von 2004 in Marousi, einem nördlichen Vorort von Athen, hinzugezogen. Sein Beitrag sind die neuen Dächer für das olympische Stadion und die Radrennbahn, Plätze und Sonnenschutzdächer für die gesamte Anlage sowie zahlreiche andere Einrichtungen. Das olympische Stadion erhält ein aus zwei gebogenen „Blättern" bestehendes Verbundglasdach über einer Fläche von 25000 Quadratmetern. Das Tragwerk jedes „Dachblattes" wird aus Doppelzangen-Stahlrohrbögen mit einer Spannweite von jeweils 304 Metern und einer Höhe von bis zu 60 Metern gebildet. Das Velodrom dagegen erhält ein aus akustischen Gründen innen mit Holz verkleidetes Metalldach mit einem Mittelfeld aus Sonnenschutz-Verbundglas. Das Dach ist 145 Meter lang, 100 Meter breit und steigt bis zu einer Höhe von 45 Metern an. Es soll die Sportler vor störenden Winden schützen. Calatrava hat auch die Freiflächen gestaltet – mit Hauptverkehrsachsen, einer von Mauern umfriedeten geschwungenen Agora, einem zentralen Platz der Nationen und Grünanlagen. Vier Eingangsbereiche bilden die öffentlichen Zugänge zum Stadionkomplex. Außerdem hat der Architekt eine 110 Meter hohe bewegliche Stahlskulptur in Form einer Spindel entworfen sowie eine „Nationenwand" – eine 250 Meter lange, 20 Meter hohe mobile Wandplastik aus Stahlrohren, die fünf Meter vom Boden abgehoben installiert wird.

Santiago Calatrava a contribué activement à la préparation des Jeux Olympiques qui se dérouleront à Marousi, dans la banlieue nord d'Athènes, en août 2004. Son intervention a porté sur les nouveaux toits du Stade olympique et vélodrome, la création de places et d'auvents pour l'ensemble du complexe ainsi que de nombreux autres équipements. Le stade olympique sera recouvert d'un toit en verre feuilleté, composé d'une paire de « feuilles » cintrées, qui couvriront 25 000 m². La structure porteuse de chaque feuille se compose d'arcs double en acier tubulaire, de 304 mètres de long de portée, qui s'élèvent à 60 mètres de haut. Le vélodrome sera abrité sous une couverture revêtue de bois à l'intérieur (pour des raisons acoustiques) et de métal à l'extérieur, la partie centrale étant en verre feuilleté traité pour la protection solaire. De 145 mètres de long, 100 mètres de large et 45 mètres de haut, il protègera les athlètes des effets gênant des vents. Calatrava travaille également sur un parc, une agora fermée tout en courbes, une place des nations, centrale, et des zones paysagées. Quatre places d'entrée faciliteront les accès au complexe olympique. L'architecte a également créé une sculpture d'acier mobile de 110 mètres de haut en forme de fuseau et un « Mur des nations » ou sculpture murale mobile en tube d'acier de 250 mètres de long et 20 mètres de haut surélevée de 5 mètres par rapport au sol.

Olympic Sports Complex,
Athens, Greece, 2001–04

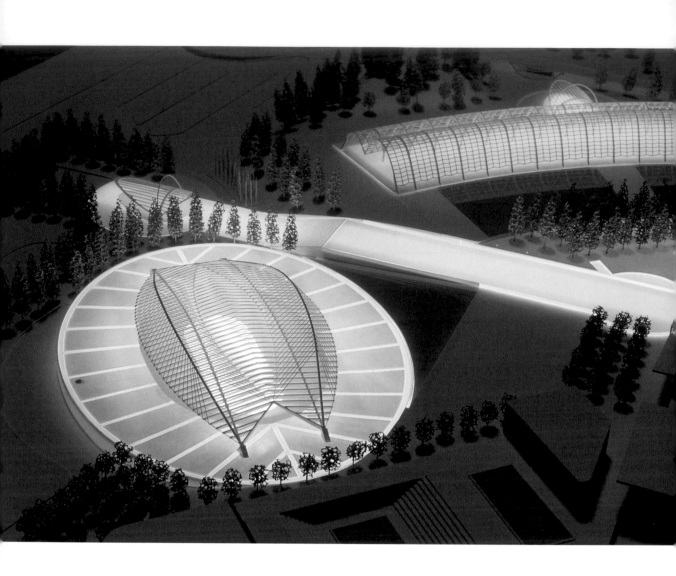

A frequent feature of the projects of Santiago Calatrava is their unexpected ability to move. As in the sculptures that he exhibits on the lawn of his Zurich atelier, this movement is undoubtedly related to his fascination for natural or anthropomorphic forms. The "frozen movement" so evident in some of his bridges, for example, here goes one step further. This was the case in the Ernsting Warehouse (Coesfeld, close to Münster, Germany, 1983–85), where the three large doors, measuring 13 by 5 meters, were designed with the joint mechanism of the human knee in mind. The hinged aluminum ribs rise to form a concave arch as they open, creating canopies. The Kuwaiti Pavilion for Expo '92 in Seville (1991–92) also integrates movement as one of its principal design features, with 17 wooden rib-like forms each 25 meters in length, which interlaced, closing during the day over a "piazza" used in the open position at night for slide and video projections. Other Calatrava projects with moving parts are the extension to the Milwaukee Art Museum, and the "Shadow Machine" (1992–93) designed for the garden of the Museum of Modern Art in New York.

La capacité au mouvement est une caractéristique fréquente et inattendue des projets de Santiago Calatrava. De même que dans les sculptures qu'il expose sur la pelouse de son atelier de Zurich, ce mouvement tient pour beaucoup à sa fascination pour les formes anthropomorphiques. Le «mouvement gelé» si évident dans certains de ses ponts, par exemple, va ici encore plus loin. C'est le cas de l'entrepôt Ernsting (Coesfeld, Allemagne, 1983–85), dont les trois grandes portes de 13 x 5 m ont été dessinées en pensant à l'articulation du genou humain. Les «côtes» d'aluminium s'ouvrent en s'élevant pour constituer un arc concave en forme de dais. Le pavillon du Koweit pour l'Expo '92 à Séville (1991–92) intègre également le mouvement dans sa conception, avec ses 17 «côtes» entrelacées en bois de 25 m de long chacune qui se referment pendant le jour sur une «piazza», et s'ouvrent la nuit pour servir d'espace de projection de diaporamas et de vidéo. Parmi les autres projets de Calatrava à éléments mobiles, figurent l'extension du Milwaukee Art Museum et sa Shadow Machine (Machine à ombres, 1992–93), dessinée pour le jardin du Museum of Modern Art de New York.

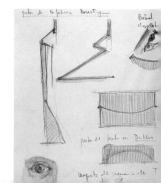

Movement

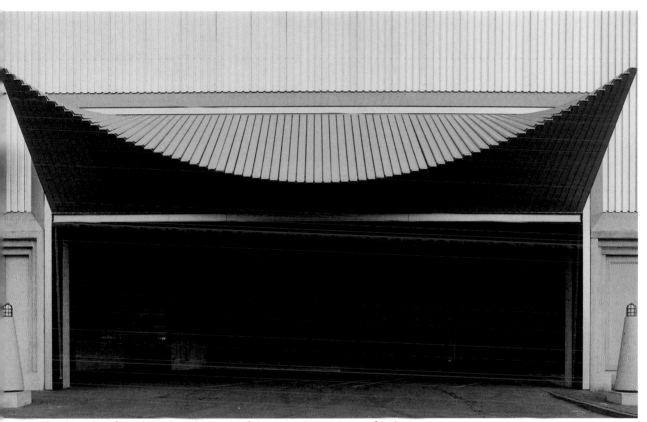

Charakteristisch für viele Werke Calatravas ist ihre unvermutete Bewegungsfähigkeit. Wie bei den Skulpturen auf dem Rasen vor Calatravas Wohnsitz in Zürich, erklärt sich diese Bewegung aus der Begeisterung des Architekten für natürliche oder anthropomorphe Formen. Der optische Eindruck der "erstarrten Bewegung", der auch in einigen Brücken Calatravas vorherrscht, wird bei seinen Skulpturen noch gesteigert. So sind zum Beispiel beim Lagerhaus der Bekleidungsfirma Ernsting in Coesfeld (westlich von Münster, 1983–85) die drei 13 mal 5 Meter großen Tore so konstruiert, daß sie an den Gelenkmechanismus des menschlichen Knies erinnern. Die drehbaren Aluminiumrippen bilden geöffnet einen Bogen, der wie ein Baldachin wirkt. Auch bei Calatravas Pavillon für Kuwait auf der Expo `92 in Sevilla (1991–92) ist das Motiv der Bewegung charakteristisch: Der Pavillon besteht aus 17 ineinander verschachtelten rippenartigen Holzformen von jeweils 25 Metern Länge, die sich während des Tages über einer »Piazza« schließen und in geöffneter Position bei Nacht für Dia- und Videoprojektionen dienen. Andere Beispiele für Bauwerke mit beweglichen Elementen sind der Erweiterungsbau des Milwaukee Art Museums oder die Skulptur »Shadow Machine« (1992–93), die er für den Garten des Museum of Modern Art in New York entwarf.

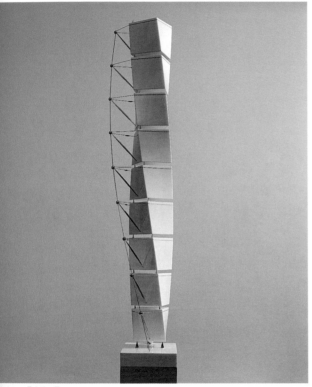

> Twisting Torso, 1991

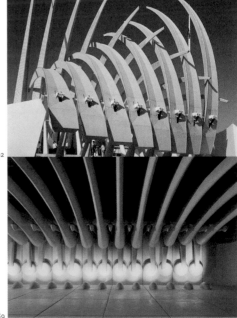

> Kuwait Pavilion 1992

> Swissbau Concrete Pavilion, 1989

> Fountain

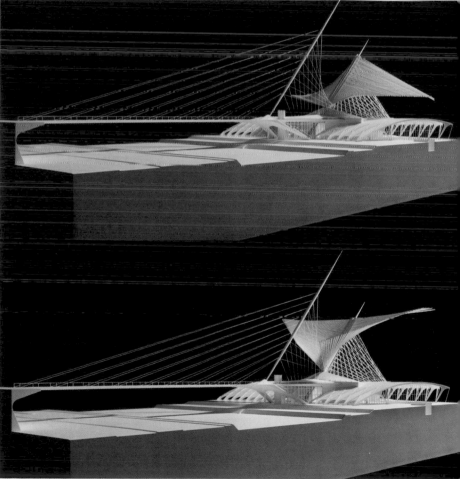

> Milwaukee Art Museum, 2001

Cable-stayed bridge studies, 1979–1981

Acleta Alpine Motor-Bridge, Disentis, Switzerland, 1979

IBA Squash Hall, Berlin, Germany, 1979

Züspa Exhibition Hall, Zurich, Switzerland, 1981

Letten Motorway Bridge, Zurich, Switzerland, 1982

Schwarzhaupt Factory, Dielsdorf, Switzerland, 1982

Mühlenareal Library, Thun, Switzerland, 1982

Rhine Bridge, Diepoldsau, Switzerland, 1982

Thalberg House Balcony Extension, Zurich, Switzerland, 1983–1983

Jakem Steel Warehouse, Munchwilen, Switzerland, 1983–1984

Ernsting's Warehouse, Coesfeld, Germany, 1983–1985

Baumwollhof Balcony, Zurich, Switzerland, 1983–1983

Stadelhofen Railway Station, Zurich, Switzerland, 1983–1990

Post Office Dispatch Roof Canopy, Lucerne, Switzerland, 1983–1985

St. Fiden Bus Stop Shelter, St. Gallen, Switzerland, 1983–1985

Wohlen Highschool, Wohlen, Switzerland, 1983–1988

Lucerne Station Hall, Lucerne, Switzerland, 1983–1989

Bärenmatte Community Centre, Suhr, Switzerland, 1984–1988

Dobi Office Building, Suhr, Switzerland, 1984–1985

De Sede Mobile Exhibition Pavilion, Zurich, Switzerland, 1984

Caballeros Footbridge, Lerida, Spain, 1984

Bach de Roda–Felipe II Bridge, Barcelona, Spain, 1984–1987

Feldenmoos Park & Ride Footbridge, Feldenmoos, Switzerland, 1

Avenida Diagonal Traffic Signals, Barcelona, Spain, 1986

9 d'Octubre Bridge, Valencia, Spain, 1986–1988

St. Gall Youth Music School Concert Room, St. Gallen, Switzerla

Blackbox Television Studio, Zurich, Switzerland, 1986–1987

Tabourettli Theatre, Basle, Switzerland, 1986–1987

Raitenau Overpass, Salzburg, Austria, 1986

BCE Place: Gallery & Heritage Square, Toronto, Canada, 1987–19

Oudry-Mesly Footbridge, Créteil-Paris, France, 1987–1988

Passerelle de Thiers, Thiers, France, 1987

Pontevedra Bridge, Pontevedra, Spain, 1987

Basarrate Underground Station, Bilbao, Spain, 1987

Alamillo Bridge and La Cartuja Viaduct, Seville, Spain, 1987–1992

Buchen Housing Estate, Würenlingen, Switzerland, 1987–1996

Banco Exterior, Zurich, Switzerland, 1987–1987

Cascine Footbridge, Florence, Italy, 1987

Pré Babel Sports Centre, Geneva, Switzerland, 1988

Leimbach Footbridge, Zurich, Switzerland, 1988

Lusitania Bridge, Merida, Spain, 1988–1991

Collserolla Television Tower, Collserolla Hills, Barcelona, Spain, 1988

Wettstein Bridge, Basle, Switzerland, 1988

Gentil Bridge, Paris, France, 1988

uschänzli Garden-Restaurant, Stadthausquai, River Limmat, Zurich, Switzerland,1988

Emergency Services Centre, Moosbruggstrasse, St. Gallen, Switzerland,1988–1999

Miraflores Bridge, Cordoba, Spain, 1989

Montjuic Telecommunications Tower, Montjuic Hill, Barcelona, Spain, 1989–1992

Bahnhofquai Tram Stop, Zurich, Switzerland, 1989

Reuss Footbridge, Flüelen, Switzerland, 1989

Swissbau Concrete Pavilion, Muba Exhibition Centre, Basle, Switzerland, 1988–1989

Bohl Covered Bus and Tram Stop, Marktplatz, St. Gall , Switzerland,1989–1996

Zurich University – Law Faculty Library, Rämi and Zürichbergstrasse, Zurich, Switzerland, 1989–

Muri Cloister Old Age Home, Muri, Switzerland, 1989

Lyon-Saint Exupéry Airport Railway Station, Satolas, Lyon, France, 1989–1994

CH-91 Floating Concrete Pavilion, Lake Lucerne, Switzerland, 1989

Gran Via Bridge, Barcelona, Spain, 1989

Nuevo acceso al puerto de Ondarroa, Ondarroa, Spain, 1989–1995

La Devesa Footbridge, Ripoll, Spain, 1989–1991

Campo Volantin Footbridge, Bilbao, Spain, 1990–1997

Spitalfields Gallery, London, Great Britain, 1990

East London River Crossing, London, England, 1990

Nouveau pont sur le Vecchio, Corsica, France, 1990

Belluard Castle Theatre, Fribourg, Switzerland, 1990

Sondica Airport, Bilbao, Spain, 1990–2000

Tenerife Concert Hall, Santa Cruz de Tenerife, Canary Islands, Spain, 1991–2003

Calabria Football Stadium, Reggio Calabria, Italy, 1991

Valencia Communications Tower, Valencia, Spain, 1991

Kuwait Pavilion, Expo'92, Seville, Spain, 1991–1992

Salou Football Stadium, Salou, Tarragona, Spain, 1991

Ciudad de las Artes y de las Ciencias, Valencia, Spain, 1991

Grand Pont Motorway Bridge, Lille, France, 1991

Alameda Bridge and Underground Station. Valencia, Spain,

Cathedral of St. John the Divine, New York, USA, 1991

Médoc Swingbridge, Bordeaux, France, 1991

Kronprinzen Bridge, Berlin, Germany, 1991–1996

Beton Forum Standard Bridge, Stockholm, Sweden, 1991

Spandau Railway Station, Spandau, Berlin, Germany, 1991

Klosterstrasse Railway Bridge, Berlin, Germany, 1991

Oberbaum Bridge Restoration, Berlin, Germany, 1991–1996

Jahn Olympic Sports Complex, Berlin, Germany, 1992

Solferino Footbridge, Paris, France, 1992

London Underground Modular Station, London, England, 1992

Tenerife Exhibition Center, Santa Cruz Tenerife, Canary Islands, 1992–1995

Reichstag Conversion, Berlin, Germany, 1992

Serreria Bridge, Valencia, Spain, 1992–

Lake Bridge, Lucerne, Switzerland, 1992

Shadow Machine, Museum of Modern Art New York, 1992–1993

Alcoy Municipal Centre, Alcoy, Spain, 1992–1995

Alcoy Bridge, Alcoy, Spain, 1992

Öresund Bridge, Copenhagen, Denmark, 1993

Ile Falcon Motorway Bridge, Sierre, Switzerland, 1993

Trinity Footbridge, Salford, England, 1993–1995

Granadilla Bridge, Tenerife, Spain, 1993

Worldcup Football Stadium, Marseille, France, 1995

Pedestrian Bridge at Turtle Bay, Redding, USA, 1995–2003

Zurich Station Platform Roof, Zurich, Switzerland, 1995

KL Linear City, Kuala Lumpur, Malaysia, 1995

Poole Harbour Bridge, Portsmouth, England, 1995

Embankment Renaissance Footbridge, Bedford, England, 1995

Sundsvall Bridge, Sundsvall, Sweden, 1995

Bilbao Football Stadium, Bilbao, Spain, 1995

Quarto Ponte sul Canale Grande, Venice, Italy, 1996–

New Olympic Stadium, Hammerby Waterfront, Stockholm, Sweden, 1996

Church of the Year 2000, Rome, Italy, 1996

Cathedral Square, Los Angeles, USA, 1996

City Point Tower, City of London, England, 1996

Mimico Creek Pedestrian Bridge, Toronto, Canada, 1996–1998

Palacio de las Artes, Valencia, Spain, 1996–2004

Service Station / Rest stop, Geneva, Switzerland, 1996

Liège Guillemins Railway Station, Liège, Belgium, 1996–

Bridge of Europe, Orléans, France, 1996–2000

Port de Barcelona, Barcelona, Spain, 1997

Barajas Airport, Madrid, Spain, 1997

Pfalzkeller Gallery, St. Gallen, Switzerland, 1997–1999

Pennsylvania Railway Station, New York, USA, 1998

Liège Pedestrian Bridge, Liège, Belgium, 1998–2000

Petach-Tikva Footbridge, Tel Aviv, Israel, 1998–2003

Rouen Bridge, Rouen, France, 1999

Cruz y Luz, Monterrey, Mexico, 1999

Zaragoza Station, Zaragoza, Spain, 1999

Residential House, Phoenix, Arizona, USA, 1999

Leuven Station, Sint-Niklaas, Belgium, 1999

Reina Sofia National Museum of Art, Madrid, Spain, 1999

Ponte sul Crati, Cosenza, Italy, 2000–

Oakland Diocese Cathedral Campus Projekt, Oakland, California, USA, 2000

Opera House Parking, Zurich, Switzerland, 2000

Dallas Fort Worth Airport, Dallas, USA, 2000

Buenavista y Jovellanos, Oviedo, Spain, 2000–

Ryerson Polytechnic University, Toronto, Canada, 2000

Darsena del Puerto, Centro Municipal, Torrevieja, Spain, 2000

Kornhaus, Rorschach, Switzerland, 2000–

Stadium Zurich, Zurich, Switzerland, 2000

SMU's Meadows Museum Sculpture Wave, Dallas, USA, 2000–2000

Ciudad de la Porcelana, Valencia, Spain, 2000–

University Campus Buildings and Sports Hall, Maastricht, The Netherlands, 2000–

The American Museum of Natural History, New York, USA, 2001

Queens Landing Pedestrian Access Improvement, Chicago, USA, 2001

Stage Setting Las Troyanas, Valencia, Spain, 2001–2001

Olympic Sports Complex, Athens, Greece, 2001–2004

Pedestrian Bridge, Athens, Greece, 2001–2004

Neratziotissa Metro and Railway Station, Athens, Greece, 2001–2004

House in Qatar, Qatar, 2001–

Bridge of Vittoria, Florence, Italy, 2002

Opera de S. Maria del Fiore, Florence, Italy, 2002–

Reggio-Emilia, Bologna, Italy, 2002–

Stage Setting Ecuba, Rome, Italy, 2002–

Light Rail Train (LRT) Bridge, Jerusalem, Israel, 2002–

Atlanta Symphony Orchestra, Atlanta, USA, 2002–

Nuovo Stazione AV di Firenze, Florence, Italy, 2002

Greenpoint Landing, New York, USA, 2002

Tower Building in Manhattan, New York, USA, 2002

Photography Museum, Doha, Qatar, 2002–

Permanent World Trade Center Path Terminal, New York, USA, 2002–

28 July 1951 Santiago Calatrava Valls, born in Valencia, Spain

1968 College graduation in Valencia

1968-1969 Attends Art School in Valencia

1969-1974 Studies architecture at the "Escuela Técnica Superior de Arquitectura de Valencia", qualification as an architect

Post-graduate Course in Urbanism

1975-1979 Studies Civil Engineering at the Swiss Federal Institute of Technology ETH Zurich

1979-1981 Doctorate in Technical Science of the Department of Architecture ETH Zurich, Ph.D. thesis: *Concerning the Foldability of Spaceframes*

Assistant at the Institute for Building Statics and Construction and for Aerodynamics and Lightweight Construction at the ETH, Zurich

1981 Architectural and engineering practice established in Zurich

1982 Membership, International Association for Bridge & Structural Engineering, Zurich

1985 9 sculptures by Santiago Calatrava, exhibition at the Jamileh Weber Gallery, Zurich

1987 Member of the BSA (Union of Swiss Architects)

Auguste Perret UIA Prize (Union Internationale d'Architectes)

Member of the International Academy of Architecture, Sofia

Participation in the *17th Triennale* in Milan

Santiago Calatrava, exhibition, Museum of Architecture, Basel

1988 City of Barcelona *Art Prize for the Bach de Roda – Felipe II Bridge*, Barcelona

Premio de la Asociación de la Prensa, (Press Association Award), Valencia

IABSE Prize, International Association of Bridge and Structural Engineering, Helsinki

FAD Prize, Fomento de las Artes y del Diseño, Spain

Fritz Schumacher Prize for Urbanism, Architecture and Engineering, Hamburg

Fazlur Rahman Khan International Fellowship for Architecture and Engineering

1989 Second architectural and engineering practice established in Paris

Honorary Member of the BDA (Bund Deutscher Architekten)

Santiago Calatrava, traveling exhibition, New York, St. Louis, Chicago, Los Angeles, Toronto, Montreal

1990 *Médaille d'Argent de la Recherche et de la Technique*, Fondation Académie d'Architecture 1970, Paris

1991 *European Glulam Award*, (Glued Laminated Timber Construction), Munich

Santiago Calatrava, exhibition, Suomen Rakennustaiteen Museum, Helsinki

City of Zurich Award for Good Building 1991, for Stadelhofen Railway Station, Zurich

Retrospective – Dynamic Equilibrium, exhibition, Museum of Design, Zurich

1992 CEOE Foundation, *VI Dragados y Construcciones Prize* for Alamillo Bridge

Honorary Member of the *Real Academia de Bellas Artes de San Carlos*, Valencia

Member of the Europe Academy, Cologne

Retrospective, exhibition, Dutch Institute for Architecture, Rotterdam

Gold Medal, Institute of Structural Engineers, London

Brunel Award, for Stadelhofen Railway Station, Zurich

Santiago Calatrava – Retrospective, exhibition, Royal Institute of British Architects, London

Retrospective, exhibition, Arkitektur Museet, Stockholm

1993 *II Honor Prize*, from the City of Pedreguer for Urban Architectonic Merit, Pedreguer

Santiago Calatrava – Bridges, exhibition, Deutsches Museum, Munich

Structure and Expression, exhibition, Museum of Modern Art (MoMA), New York

Hon RIBA Honorary Member of the Royal Institute of British Architects, London

Santiago Calatrava, exhibition, La Lontja Museum, Valencia

Santiago Calatrava, exhibition, Overbeck Society Pavilion, Lübeck

Santiago Calatrava, exhibition, Architecture Centre, Gammel Dok, Copenhagen

Doctor Honoris Causa, Polytechnic University of Valencia

Medalla de Honor al Fomento de la Invención, Fundación García Cabrerizo, Madrid

City of Toronto Urban Design Award, for the BCE Place Galeria, Toronto

World Economic Forum Davos honours Santiago Calatrava as *Global Leader for Tomorrow*

1994 *Santiago Calatrava – Recent Projects*, exhibition, Bruton Street Gallery, London

Doctor Honoris Causa, University of Seville

Santiago Calatrava – Buildings and Bridges, exhibition, Museum of Applied and Folk Arts, Moscow

Creu de Sant Jordi, Generalitat de Catalunya, Barcelona

Doctor Honoris Causa of Letters in Environmental Studies, Heriot-Watt University, Edinburgh

Santiago Calatrava – The Dynamics of Equilibrium, exhibition, Ma Gallery, Tokio

Santiago Calatrava, exhibition, Arqueria de los Nuevos Ministerios, Madrid

Santiago Calatrava, exhibition, Sala de Arte "La Recova", Santa Cruz de Tenerife

Fellow Honoris Causa, The Royal Incorporation of Architects, Scotland

Honorary Member of Colegio de Arquitectos, City of Mexico

Maître D'Oeuvre, Grande halle de la gare TGV Lyon-Saint Exupéry Airport, Rhône

1995 *Santiago Calatrava*, exhibition, Centro Cultural de Belem, Lisbon

Santiago Calatrava – Construction and Movement, exhibition, Fondazione Angelo Masieri, Venice

Doctor Honoris Causa of Science, University College, Salford

Santiago Calatrava, exhibition, Navarra Museum, Pamplona

Canton of Lucerne, *Award for Good Building 1983-1993*, for the railway station and square

Certificate for the Practice of Professional Engineering, Frosinone

1996 *Medalla de Oro al Mérito de las Bellas Artes*, Ministry of Culture, Granada

Santiago Calatrava, exhibition, Archivo Foral, Bilbao

Santiago Calatrava, Bewegliche Architekturen – bündel fächer welle, exhibition, Museum of Design, Zurich

Santiago Calatrava – opere e progetti 1980-1996, exhibition, Palazzo della Ragione, Padova

Mostra Internazionale di Scultura All'aperto, exhibition, Vira Gambarogno, Ascona, Bellinzona

Doctor Honoris Causa of Science, University of Strathclyde, Glasgow

Santiago Calatrava – Quatro Ponte sul Canal Grande, exhibition, Spazio Olivetti, Venice

Santiago Calatrava – Sculpture, exhibition, Government Building, St. Gallen

Santiago Calatrava – Kunst ist Bau – Bau ist Kunst, exhibition, Department of Building, Basel

Santiago Calatrava, exhibition, Milwaukee Art Museum, Milwaukee, Wisconsin

Santiago Calatrava – City Point

A New Tower for the City, exhibition, Britannic Tower, London

1997 *Doctor Honoris Causa of Science*, University of Technology, Delft

Santiago Calatrava – Structures and Movement, exhibition, National Museum of Science, Haifa

European Award for Steel Structures, reconstruction of the "Kronprinzenbrücke", Berlin

Louis Vuitton – Moet Hennessy Art Prize, Paris

Master de Oro del Forum de Alta Dirección, Madrid

Doctor Honoris Causa of Engineering, Milwaukee School of Engineering, Milwaukee, Wisconsin

Structural Engineer Licence by the State of Illinois Department of Professional Engineering, Licence No. 081-005441, granted November (Renewed in 1998 and 2000)

Temporary *Licence for the Practice of Professional Engineering* by the State of California Board of Professional Engineers and Land Surveyors (Renewed in 1998)

1998 Member of *Les Arts et Lettres*, Paris

Santiago Calatrava – Work in Progress, exhibition, Triennale in Milan

1998 Brunel Award for the Oriente Station, Lisbon Multimodal Station S.A. Portugal

Lecture series for the School of Architecture and Design at Massachusetts Institute of Technology, Boston

Lecture series Winter semester, Architecture Department, ETH Zurich

1999 *Doctor Honoris Causa of Civil Engineering*, Università degli Studi di Cassino

Principe de Asturias, Art Prize, Spain

Doctor Honoris Causa of Technology, University of Lund

Foreign Member of the Academy, Royal Swedish Academy of Engineering Sciences, IVA

Licence for the Practice of Professional Engineering by the State of Texas, Board of Professional Engineers, Licence No. 85263

Grau Grande Oficial da Ordem do Mérito, Chancelaria das Ordens Honorificas Portuguesas, Lisbon

Gold Medal, The Concrete Society, London

Honorable Mention, Canadian Consulting Engineering Awards for the Mimico Creek Bridge, Toronto

Santiago Calatrava, Traveling Exhibition, Montevideo, Buenos Aires

Doctor Honoris Causa of Architecture, Universita degli Studi di Ferrara

Honorary Fellowship, Royal Architectural Institute of Canada College of Fellows

"Das Goldene Dach 2000", The Golden Roof, Structural Completion of the "Pfalzkeller", St. Gallen

Fellowship, Institute for Urban Design, New York
Honorary Fellowship, National Academy of Architecture, Monterrey
Lecture Series for the School of Architecture and Design at Massachusetts Institute of Technology, Boston
Guest of Honour, Mexico City, D.F. Government
Santiago Calatrava Scultore, Ingegnere, Architetto, Palazzo Strozzi, Florence
Beauty and Efficiency, a Challenge of Modern Infrastructure, The IVA Royal Technology Forum, Stockholm
2000 *Algur H. Meadows Award for Excellence in the Arts*, Meadows School of Arts, Dallas
Temporary *Licence and Certificate of Practice for Engineering*, OAA Ontario Association of Architects
Gold Medal, Círculo de Bellas Artes, Valencia
Honorary Academician, Real Academia de Bellas Artes de San Fernando, Madrid
Prize Exitos 2000 to the best architectural work for the Science Museum in Valencia, Madrid

Calatrava Architect, Sculptor, Engineer, Exhibition, National Gallery Alexandros Soutzos Museum, Athens
Calatrava Poetics of Movement, Exhibition, Meadows Museum Southern Methodist University, Dallas
Award for Excellence in Design for the Time Capsule, American Museum of Natural History, New York
Temporary Licence for the Practice of Professional Engineering by the State of Wisconsin Board of Architects, Landscape Architects, Professional Engineers, Designers and Land Surveyors
Santiago Calatrava Esculturas y Dibujos, Exhibition, IVAM Centre Julio González, Valencia
Calatrava XX/XXI, Exhibition, Form and Design Center, Malmö
European Award for Steel Structures for the Europe Bridge over the Loire River, Orléans
Calatrava, Exhibition, Teloglion Foundation, Thessaloniki

2002 *Best of 2001 Prize* for the design of the Milwaukee Art Museum Extension, *Time Magazine*, New York
Prize *"Il Principe e L'Architetto"* for the design of the Quarto Ponte sul Canal Grande in Venice, Architettura e Design per la Città, Bologna
Prize *The Sir Misha Black Medal*, Royal College of Art, London
Prize *2002 The Best Large Structural Project* for the Milwaukee Art Museum Addition, The Structural Engineers Association of Illinois
Santiago Calatrava, Traveling Exhibition, Palacio de Minería, Mexico City, Museo de Arte Moderno, Santo Domingo
The Leonardo da Vinci Medal, by the SEFI for having made an outstanding contribution of international significance to engineering education, SEFIRENZE 2000, Florence.
2003 *Medalla al Mérito a las Bellas Artes*, Real Academia de San Carlos de Valencia, Valencia

Bibliography > Bibliographie

Santiago Calatrava : Il folle volo / The daring flight. Pierluigi Nicolin, Electa, Milano, 1987
Santiago Calatrava: Engenieur-Architektur. Werner Blaser, Birkhäuser, Basel, 1987
Santiago Calatrava 1983 / 1989. Richard C. Levene, Fernando Marquez Cecilia; El Croquis, Madrid, 1989
Ein Bahnof / Une gare – Archithese. Bernhard Klein, Kenneth Frampton, Lukas Schmutz, Peter Rice, Arthur Niggli, Heiden, 1990
Dynamische Gleichgewichte Neue Projekte – Dynamic Equilibrium Recent Projects – Santiago Calatrava. Artemis, Zürich, 1991
Creatures from the Mind of the Engineer – The Architecture of Santiago Calatrava. Robert Harrison; Artemis, Zürich, 1992
Santiago Calatrava. Exhibition Catalogue Museum für Gestaltung, Anthony C. Webster, Kenneth Frampton, Zürich, 1992
Santiago Calatrava. Exhibition Catalogue, Dennis Sharp, London, 1992
Santiago Calatrava – Structure and Expression. Exhibition Catalogue Museum of Modern Art, Matilda McQuaid, New York, 1992
Calatrava Bridges. Kenneth Frampton, Anthony C. Webster, Anthony Tischhauser; Birkhäuser, Basel, 1993
Santiago Calatrava – Bahnhof Stadelhofen, Zurich. Bernhard Klein; Ernst Wasmuth, Tübingen, Berlin, 1993
Santiago Calatrava 1983–1993. Exhibition Catalogue, El Croquis, Madrid, 1993
Calatrava : Escale à Satolas. Marianne Le Roux, Michel Rivoire; Editions Glénat, Grenoble, 1994

Calatrava Berlin : Five Projects / Fünf Projekte. Michael S. Cullen, Martin Kieren; Birkhäuser, Basel, 1994
Calatrava Escale Satolas. Gallery MA, Glénat, Grenoble, 1994
Santiago Calatrava –The Dynamics of Equilibrium. Exhibition Catalogue, Tokyo, 1994
Gobernio de Navarra – Santiago Calatrava. Exhibition Catalogue, Musco de Navarra, 1995
Movement, Structure and the work of Santiago Calatrava. Alexander Tzonis, Liane Lefaivre; Birkhäuser, Basel, 1995
Santiago Calatrava – Building and Bridges. Europa Akademie, Federico Motta Editore, Milano, 1995
Santiago Calatrava – Secret Sketchbook. Mirco Zardini; Federico Motta Editore, Milano, 1995
Architectural Monographs N° 46 – Santiago Calatrava. Dennis Sharp; Academy Editions, London, 1996
Santiago Calatrava. Exhibition Catalogue, Galerie Jamileh Weber, Wolfau-Druck Rudolf Mühlemann, Weinfelden, Valencia, 1996
Santiago Calatrava. Exhibition Catalogue, Generalitat Valenciana, Valencia, 1996
Santiago Calatrava – Complete Works. Exhibition Catalogue, Sergio Polano, Electa, Milano, 1996
Santiago Calatrava 1983–1996, AV Monografías / Monographs 61 (1996). Luis Fernandes-Galiano; Arquitectura Viva, Madrid, 1996
Santiago Calatrava – Progetti e Opere. Mario Pisani, Enrico Sicignano; Domizia Mandolesi, Roma, 1997
Santiago Calatrava - Structures and Movement.

Exhibition Catalogue, Rifca Hashimshony, Haifa, 1997
Oriente Station. Philip Jodidio; Centralivros Lda., Lisbon, 1998
Santiago Calatrava. Exhibition Catalogue, Luca Molinari, Skira, Milano, 1998
Santiago Calatrava: Public Buildings. Anthony Tischhauser, Stanislaus von Moos; Birkhäuser, Basel, 1998
Santiago Calatrava. Catalogue of the exhibition of Montevideo, Manuel Blanco, Generalitat Valenciana, 1999
Santiago Calatrava – The Poetics of Movement. Alexander Tzonis; Universe Publishing, New York, 1999
Calatrava – Drawings and Sculptures. Michael Levin; Wolfau-Druck Rudolf Mühlemann, Weinfelden, 2000
Santiago Calatrava – Sculptures in Movement. Catalogue of the exhibition of Dallas, Meadows Museum, 2001
Sculptures and Drawings – Esculturas y dibujos. IVAM Catalogue of the exhibition of Valencia, Generalitat Valenciana, Valencia, 2001
Santiago Calatrava. Conversations with Students. Cecilia Lewis Kausel, Ann Pendleton-Jullian; Princeton Architectural Press, 2002
Santiago Calatrava. Artworks. Michael Levin; Birkhäuser, Basel, 2003
Santiago Calatrava. Wie ein Vogel / Like a Bird. Liane Lefaivre; Skira, Genève / Milano, 2003